D1554263

TREASURES IN THE SAND

ORLEY BERG

What archeology tells us about the Bible

TREASURES IN THE SAND

ORLEY BERG

Pacific Press Publishing Association
Boise, Idaho
Oshawa, Ontario, Canada

Edited by Jerry D. Thomas
Designed by Dennis Ferree
Cover art by Lars Justinen
Typeset in 10.5/12.5 Century Schoolbook

Copyright © 1993 by
Pacific Press Publishing Association
Printed in United States of America
All Rights Reserved

Library of Congress Cataloging-in-Publication Data:
Berg, Orley.
    Treasures in the sand : what archaeology tells us about the Bible
/ Orley Berg.
        p.   cm.
    Includes bibliographical references.
    ISBN 0-8163-1110-2
    1. Bible—Antiquities. 2. Bible—Evidences, authority, etc.
I. Title.
BS621.B47   1993
220.9'3—dc20
                                                    92-14845
                                                        CIP

93 94 95 96 97 ● 5 4 3 2 1

Contents

Introduction

An Egyptian peasant, working in her garden on the island of Elephantine, comes across some old parchments. They turn out to be from the time of Ezra and Nehemiah, offering significant data on that period of Israel's history.

A youthful twenty-four-year-old Italian archaeologist begins to dig at a mound in Syria. After ten fruitless years, he uncovers the capital city of Ebla, with an ancient library of twenty thousand tablets and fragments dating back to the third millennium B.C. It opens up an entirely new world of study.

A lone archaeologist, working among old tablets from Nineveh, suddenly finds himself reading about a great flood. Although there are differences, the amazing similarities make it obvious that this is a record of the same flood that Noah survives in the book of Genesis.

So the story of archaeological discovery unfolds. It covers a period of 191 years, from the discovery of the Rosetta Stone in 1799 and its deciphering in 1822 to the excavation of the magnificent palace of Esarhaddon, son of Sennacherib, at Nineveh in the spring of 1990.

These treasures in the sand have illuminated every period of biblical history. Diggings such as those at Ur of the Chaldees, Mari, and Ebla have given us a striking picture of the high civilization that was home to the patriarch Abraham until he followed his God to a new land.

Amazing discoveries in Egypt and Sinai have cast new light on the period of Israel's sojourn in Egypt and the Exodus. Ancient tablets from Sinai and Ras Shamrah have confirmed the existence of an alphabetic script Moses could have used in the writing of the first books of the Bible. The name of

"Balaam, the son of Beor," has recently come to light. Excavations at Shechem have uncovered what is believed to be the altar constructed by Joshua.

Critics of the Bible once questioned the existence of the kings of Israel and Judah mentioned in the Bible. Now, the names of twelve of them have been found written on ancient tablets of clay.

Excavations at Nineveh and the surrounding region have uncovered no less than five Assyrian palaces. Four of them belonged to kings mentioned in the Scriptures, confirming significant details given in the Bible.

Critics who challenged the reliability of the book of Daniel have been amazed to discover how wrong they were. Nebuchadnezzar emerges from the archaeological dust as a great builder and king, just as portrayed in the book of Daniel. Belshazzar was truly king of Babylon, as vice-regent with his father, Nabonidus, at the time of the fall of the city, contrary to what the critics had claimed.

Recent excavations in Jerusalem have uncovered debris left by Nebuchadnezzar's destructive invasion. From the ashes have come the names of Jeremiah's trusted scribe and contemporaries mentioned in his book. The name of Judah's captive king, Jehoiachin, has been found among the chronicles of Babylon.

The Elephantine Papyri that were found by the Egyptian peasant identify Sanballat, Nehemiah's great adversary, as the governor of Samaria. Recorded in those same ancient writings is a letter from the Jews of Egypt to Johanan, high priest at Jerusalem, frequently referred to in the book of Nehemiah, requesting permission to build a sanctuary.

The uncovering of these buried treasures is a thrilling story. In this exciting period of history, one discovery after another helps to broaden our understanding of the Bible and confirm its divine authorship. So travel with me through time as we see the people of the Bible in the light of archaeology. In that world of ancient mysteries and hidden treasures, our adventure begins.

Chapter 1

Where History Began

Let's travel back to the beginning of history as we know it, to the cradle of civilization. The first people of which we have any knowledge occupied two main areas: the Nile River valley and delta in Egypt, and the plain between the Tigris and Euphrates rivers in Mesopotamia. Between these two populated areas lies the land bridge of Syria and Palestine.

James H. Breasted, the famous Egyptologist, described this area as a huge crescent and coined the phrase "Fertile Crescent," a name by which it is still known. Above the crescent are rugged mountains; below it, vast stretches of desert.

The Nile River runs through the heart of Egypt and forms the lower portion of this fertile crescent. Oddly, northern Egypt is called Lower Egypt, because, unlike most rivers, the Nile runs from south to north. So to go down the Nile is to go north—to Lower Egypt; and to go up the Nile is to go south—to Upper Egypt. The lower crescent gave birth to one of the first great cities—Memphis, in Lower Egypt.

Mesopotamia means "between the rivers." This upper portion of the Fertile Crescent was well watered by a vast system of canals and ditches. Canal building was a major industry—like road construction today. With ample water and sunshine, this rich land became a great center of agriculture. During the fourteenth century, however, the canal system was willfully destroyed by Jamerlane, and the fields became the desert that we see today.

It is said that Egypt is the gift of the Nile. Ninety-two percent of Egypt's population lives on 3 percent of its soil—the area watered by this mighty river. Without the Nile, there would never have been the great Egyptian civilization of antiquity.

In the same way, Mesopotamia is the gift of the Tigris and the Euphrates. These two great rivers have their source far up in the central mountains of Turkey. Flowing down toward the Persian Gulf, they carry and deposit silt that has built up the land through the centuries. Without these rivers, much of the land area we see today would not even exist. For instance, in the days of Abraham, the city of Ur was situated near the Persian Gulf. Today the site is 160 miles inland.

At the very dawn of history, Mesopotamia was populated by the earth's first civilized inhabitants. Most of what was ancient Mesopotamia is today in Iraq. To its earliest peoples, the area was known as "the land of Sumer," so its civilization is known as the Sumerian civilization.

It is remarkable that a century ago, we knew nothing of this civilization. No one even imagined that such a civilization existed. It had completely vanished from history and was lost for more than three thousand years. Then came the amazing discovery of the Sumerian race by archaeologists.

The languages of ancient civilizations recovered

The science of archaeology was born in 1798, during the days of Napoleon. In that year he invaded Egypt, taking with him 120 scholars who were instructed to search the land for whatever antiquities it might have to offer. His greatest find was the now famous Rosetta Stone. This single discovery is said to be more important for ancient history than are all the inventions of Thomas Edison for modern life.

The Rosetta Stone is inscribed with three languages: Greek and two Egyptian scripts, the hieroglyphic and the demotic

Egyptian, a cursive form of writing simpler than hieroglyphics. Although the Greek could be read, the Egyptian language had been dead and forgotten for two thousand years. Since the same message was inscribed in three scripts and two languages, scholars compared the Egyptian language with the Greek, and the demotic and hieroglyphic scripts were deciphered. Their decipherment made it possible to read the many mysterious inscriptions covering the vast temples and tomb chambers of Egypt. It revolutionized our knowledge of the long-lost peoples and civilizations of the land of the pharaohs.

While the history of ancient Egypt was being rediscovered, something was also happening in Mesopotamia. For many long centuries, travelers had walked beneath the towering cliffs of the Behistun Rock, in present-day Iran. They had often paused to gaze at the strange reliefs carved on a great stone surface five hundred feet above their reach. Like the Rosetta Stone, the Behistun Rock, too, was inscribed in three languages—but *all three* had been lost.

In 1835, Henry Rawlinson, a British official and a remarkable scholar, was stationed near this gigantic rock. For four years, working when he could, he produced replicas of the strange inscriptions. He did this while standing on a narrow ledge, on the steps of a ladder, or let down by ropes, often at the risk of his life. Six years of study followed and resulted in the amazing decipherment of the Old Persian and Elamite and later the Babylonian cuneiform, making it possible to read the exploits of the long-lost peoples and nations of Mesopotamia.

The word *cuneiform* means "wedge-shaped," which accurately describes the characters used in these ancient languages. Using this wedge-shaped writing, the Persian king, Darius I "the Great" (521-486 B.C.), had reliefs and inscriptions celebrating his victory over rebel tribes carved on the face of the Behistun Rock cliff.

Bringing buried civilizations to life
Rawlinson's work led explorers to search for the ancient

cities of Mesopotamia. They soon found that Mesopotamia is a vast cemetery. From a single spot, you can sometimes see as many as three great artificial mounds, known as tells, rise out of the desert landscape. The natives who pitched their tents near them or watered their camels in their shadows never knew, but beneath each of the mounds lay the remains of cities and civilizations.

In this respect, Egypt is vastly different from Mesopotamia. Egypt was built with stone. Its massive stone structures of antiquity still amaze the tourists. In Mesopotamia, there was little or no stone, so the inhabitants built with clay bricks. Such buildings were easily destroyed by natural causes—floods, earthquakes, and storms of wind and rain. But most often, the cities were destroyed by war. A city defeated in war and partially destroyed was often leveled off so that another could be built over it. In this way, the mounds grew like a layer cake.

As the archaeologists dig down, the layers are peeled off one after another, sometimes as many as twenty or more of them. Most of the buildings were constructed with sun-dried bricks, which easily disintegrate. The outside layer of the walls, however, would often be made of oven-baked bricks. These much more durable bricks were not used extensively because the fuel it took to bake them was limited.

The world's great cities uncovered

Of particular interest to the archaeologists were the mounds in the area of Mosul, 220 miles north of Baghdad. There they hoped to find the ancient city of Nineveh. Nineveh was destroyed in 612 B.C., and with the passing of time, even the site where it had stood was forgotten.

In 1843, P. E. Botta, a Frenchman, began to dig at Khorsabad, fifteen miles north of Mosul. He uncovered the remains of a great Assyrian palace. Jubilantly, he sent word to Paris that Nineveh had been found. But instead, he had discovered the ancient city of Dur-Sarrukin, and the palace was that of Sargon II of the eighth century B.C.

Two years later, while Botta continued his work at Khorsabad, an Englishman, Austin Henry Layard, began digging with amazing success at Nimrud, twenty-four miles south of Mosul. He uncovered parts of three fabulous palaces, and he was certain he had found Nineveh. But the site was later identified as the ancient city of Calah, one of the earliest cities mentioned in the Bible,[1] built during the early period after the construction of the tower of Babel.

Switching to the mound of Kuyunjik, two miles up the Tigris from Mosul, Layard came up with an even more startling result. He uncovered the great palace of Sennacherib of biblical fame.[2] Sennacherib (705-681 B.C.) was the son of Sargon, and his palace was in Nineveh. The elusive lost city had been found.

New light from an ancient library at Nineveh

The earliest writing was on clay tablets. If the tablets were hardened in fire, they were almost indestructible—more durable than iron or brass, since metals corrode.

Letters or documents would often be placed inside envelopes that were also made of clay. The envelope would carry the name of the sender and indicate the person to whom it was sent.[3] Because of the high value placed on writing, the scribal schools and libraries were among the most important aspects of a palace.

The most significant find at Nineveh came when the palace of Ashurbanipal (669-626 B.C.) was uncovered. Its fantastic remains included the king's great library, packed with twenty thousand clay tablets on almost every subject under the sun, and all were filed according to subject.

Scholars were overwhelmed. A whole new world suddenly opened before them, for the king had gathered tablets from all the nations comprising his vast empire. The tablets, of all shapes and sizes, were inscribed with the now familiar wedge-shaped cuneiform characters.

Many of the tablets found in Ashurbanipal's palace at Nineveh were in the already deciphered Akkadian language and were easily read. Others, however, were different. They were inscribed with a language that was totally new, although the same wedge-shaped characters were used.

In the Akkadian texts, there was frequent mention of the "king of Sumer and Akkad." Sumer was a name no one had read before. Gradually, the story of the Sumerian civilization came to light.

Sumerian tablets by the thousands were found, most of them dating to the latter part of the third millennium B.C. (about 2750 B.C.). These included bilingual texts that helped scholars to decipher the Sumerian language. In 1914, the first Sumerian grammar was published. As the scholarly world looked on, the amazing history of this civilization was unfolded.

In the Bible, the area of Sumer is called "the land of Shinar."[4] Both the Bible and the ancient library of Ashurbanipal point to Sumer in Mesopotamia as the birthplace of civilization. As one writer states it, "History begins at Sumer."

The world's first civilization

The Sumerian civilization developed the first effective system of writing, the first schools, the first congress, the first tax cut, the first law code, the first pharmacopoeia (the preparation of salves for healing), the first "Farmer's Almanac," and the first animal fables.[5]

Since the scribes enjoyed the prestige of one of the most important professions, the formal system of education provided special classes for them. Courses in law were also offered. The famous Code of Hammurabi was once thought to be the oldest law code in existence. We now have the Sumer law code, which is five hundred years older.

Physicians were also in demand. The oldest known prescription by a doctor, a Sumerian, comes from the third millennium B.C.

The Sumerians were the first to develop cylinder seals. The cylinders were rolled over soft clay, leaving a unique, official seal on a document.

The Sumerians were conquered about 2400 B.C. by the Akkadians, but their culture was retained, as were their cuneiform writing characters. Three hundred years later, the Sumerians regained their independence. But when the Babylonians under the great king Hammurabi began to rule the world, the Sumerians disappeared from history and were lost and forgotten until modern times.

The excavations at Nippur

Among the most significant and extensive excavations of the Sumerian culture are those at Nippur, one hundred miles south of Baghdad. The centennial observance of the work there was held in 1988. Excavations had began one hundred years before by the University of Pennsylvania museum of Philadelphia. J. P. Peters and others dug for three years, turning up some thirty thousand tablets and fragments. Unfortunately, it would be fifty years before they were analyzed carefully. This remarkable task was finally undertaken by Dr. Samuel Noah Kramer, who devoted a good share of his life to their study.[6]

The tablets revealed an amazing skill in arts and crafts, massive building enterprises, and a very advanced system of irrigation. Four thousand of the tablets are of a literary nature, relating religious mythology, epics, hymns, and proverbs.

Of special interest are the many tablets that throw light on the Bible. Here was a library of information relating to humans' earliest history, a period about which absolutely nothing was known before except what was recorded in the Old Testament Scriptures.

The Bible as history

Few realize how deeply we are indebted to the Bible for

what we know of ancient history. The Bible is the only record of the ancient world that has remained available through the ages. Without it, ancient history would at one time have been a blank. The only other sources available were the records of a few Greek and Latin writers like Herodotus, but they do not go back beyond the fifth or sixth centuries B.C. And at that time the great civilizations of Egypt and Mesopotamia were already in their last stages.

Many are surprised to learn that, were it not for the Bible, the science of archaeology might never have been born. What motivated the early explorers? Why did Botta, Layard, and their successors go looking for Nineveh, Babylon, and other lost cities? Because they read of them in the Bible. Nineveh is mentioned twenty times in the Scriptures, and Babylon is mentioned three hundred times or more.

Why did foreigners always do the digging? Why always the French, British, Germans, Americans, and others? Why not the native inhabitants—those who lived there? Because, without a knowledge of the Bible, they knew little or nothing of those cities. They had no interest in them. They wouldn't have known what to look for. So when the foreigners came, the inhabitants were certain they had come to search for treasures of gold.

Is Bible history reliable?

Because we recognize the importance of history, we can understand the importance of the Bible and its contribution to our knowledge of the ancient world. But that leaves a big question: Is Bible history reliable?

Throughout the Christian era, the Bible was generally accepted for what it claimed to be, the divinely inspired Word of God. But with the rise of higher criticism and the skeptical age of the nineteenth century, all this changed. One Bible book after another was challenged, until by 1875 there was scarcely a scholar left who accepted the Bible as true history. To them, it was but a compilation of legends and myths.

In God's providence, the science of archaeology was born at

the very time the Bible was being challenged and verification was so much needed. The science of archaeology made it possible to compare the hundreds and thousands of ancient texts with the Bible. Ancient languages, long forgotten, were rediscovered. Inscribed tablets, buried for thousands of years, began to cry out. Lost cities and civilizations were unearthed from their lonely mounds. And what a story they had to tell!

The massive remains of Egypt confirmed the Bible record. For countless centuries people in Egypt viewed the inscribed walls of temples and tombs, were intrigued by their mysterious reliefs, and wondered at their secrets. Now they could read and interpret them. On the outer wall of the great hypostyle hall of Karnak, they could now identify the huge figure as Pharaoh Shishak, known previously from the Bible. They could now read of his exploits into Palestine, which were written on the temple wall, as well as in the Scriptures,[7] and both were in perfect agreement.

The unearthed Mesopotamian palaces proved to belong to Assyrian kings often named in the Scriptures. Scholars once questioned the existence of King Sargon. They knew nothing of him except for the reference in Isaiah 20:1. Then came the discovery of his palace at Khorsabad. The palace walls were covered with fascinating reliefs, some of them even speaking of events also mentioned in the Bible. King Sargon of the Bible became an actual figure of history—the first instance of ancient texts confirming a biblical statement.

The science of archaeology has convincingly established the reliability and the reality of Bible history.

---

1. Genesis 10:11.
2. 2 Kings 18:13–19:37; 2 Chronicles 32:1-22.
3. See Edward Chiera, *They Wrote on Clay* (University of Chicago Press, 1938, 1966).
4. Genesis 10:10; 11:2; Daniel 1:2.
5. Samuel N. Kramer, "Sumerian 'Firsts'," *Biblical Archaeological Review (BAR)*, September/October 1984, 62, 63.
6. Since 1948 the Oriental Institute of the University of Chicago has been on the site until forced out by the crisis brought on by Iraq's invasion of Kuwait in early August 1990.
7. 1 Kings 14:25, 26.

Chapter 2

Creation, the Flood, and the Tower of Babel

As mentioned in the last chapter, a major breakthrough came with the discovery of the vast library of Ashurbanipal at Nineveh. The king had originals, or copies, of just about everything of importance that had survived to his time. To officials everywhere he had sent out the urgent message:

> "Seek out and bring to me the precious tablets for which there are no transcripts extant in Assyria. . . . If you hear of any tablet or ritualistic text that is suitable for the palace, seek it out, secure it, and send it here."[1]

The tablets dealt with history, science, religion, and economics. There were official dispatches, business documents, and letters of all sorts, along with dictionaries and grammars of the various languages.

The story of Creation

Of the many tablets that had a direct relationship to the Bible, seven told the story of Creation. The Babylonian version from the library of Ashurbanipal at Nimrud was an update of the earlier Sumerian accounts found at Nippur.

Although the seven creation tablets differ from the biblical version, there are many striking similarities: Both ascribe origins to direct creation—there is not a hint of evolution. Both speak of a time when the earth was waste and void. Both give a similar order to the events of creation. Both favor the number seven—seven days, seven tablets.

But there are also differences. The Bible pictures one God, lofty and sublime, supreme, omnipotent, in control. There is a great difference between Him and His creatures. The tablets describe many gods, and they are wicked, selfish, conniving, accusing. Man was created from the blood of the slain god Kingu. Half of the slain goddess Tiamat became the sky; the other half became the earth.

The question naturally arises, Which came first, the Babylonian account or the Genesis account?

There are three possibilities:

1. *The Genesis account was taken from the Babylonian account.* But it is very unlikely that the pure, lofty account of creation in the Bible would have been sifted out of the immoral, debased, legendary myths of the Babylonians. Stories like these myths are usually just the opposite; pure, original stories becoming more distorted and corrupt with the passage of time.

2. *The Babylonian account was drawn from the Genesis account.* This is impossible, for the Genesis story was written down a thousand years after the Babylonian account was written.

3. *Both the Genesis account and the Babylonian account arose spontaneously from a common source.* This is unquestionably what happened. As Merril Unger, the noted scholar, puts it:

> They are traditions common to all civilized nations of antiquity. Their common elements point to a time when the human race occupied a common home and held a common faith. Their likenesses are due to a common

inheritance, each race of men handing on from age to age records, oral and written, of the primeval history of the race.[2]

What about Noah's flood?

In 1872, in the basement of the British Museum, George Smith was working on some of the tablets from Ashurbanipal's famous library. His eyes fell on some lines that engaged his profound attention. Almost unbelieving, he read:

I looked about for coast lines in the expanse of the sea:
in each of fourteen (regions)
There emerged a region (mountain).
On Mount Nisir the ship came to a halt.
Mount Nisir held the ship fast,
    Allowing no motion.
One day, a second day, Mount Nisir held the ship fast,
    Allowing no motion.
A third day, a fourth day, Mount Nisir held the ship fast,
    Allowing no motion.
A fifth, and a sixth (day), Mount Nisir held the ship fast,
    Allowing no motion.
When the seventh day arrived,
I sent forth and set free a dove.
The dove went forth, but came back;
Since no resting-place for it was visible, she turned round.[3]

Reporting on his find, Smith declared: "It is apparent that the events of the flood narrated in the Bible and the inscriptions are the same and occur in the same order."

The flood tablet Smith was reading originated in the days of Hammurabi when Babylon rose to power, but, like the Creation story, was an update of an earlier Sumerian account from Nippur. It was a part of what is known as the Gilgamesh Epic. The floods come, and Utnapishtin, the great hero, survives in a great boat. A dove, then a swallow, and finally a raven are sent out. Utnapishtin then offers sacrifices and explains how he received eternal life.

A further sampling from this tablet reads as follows:

Tear down (this) house, build a ship!
Give up possessions, seek thou life.
Forswear (worldly) goods and keep the soul alive!
Aboard the ship take thou the seed of all living things.
. . .
All my family and kin I made go aboard the ship.
The beasts of the field, the wild creatures of the field,
    All the craftsmen I made go aboard. . . .
I watched the appearance of the weather.
The weather was awesome to behold.
I boarded the ship and battened up the entrance. . . .
The gods were frightened by the deluge,
And, shrinking back, they ascended to the heaven of Anu.
The gods cowered like dogs. . . .
I looked at the weather: stillness had set in,
And all of mankind had returned to clay. . . .
[Here follow the lines first read by Smith.]
Then I let out (all) to the four winds
    And offered a sacrifice.
I poured out a libation on the top of the mountain.[4]

The introduction of the earlier Sumerian account, of which the Gilgamesh Epic was an update, includes the words,

By my hand shall a deluge be sent upon the . . .
The seed of mankind shall perish in destruction.
This is the decision, the command of the assembly of the gods.[5]

A comparison of the Babylonian Gilgamesh account of the flood with the Bible account reveals many similarities:

1. The deluge was divinely planned.
2. The plan was divinely revealed to the hero.
3. The hero was divinely instructed to build a large boat.
4. The hero and family were delivered from the deluge.
5. Both accounts indicate the physical causes of the flood.
6. Both accounts indicate a specific length of time for the flood.
7. Both give the name of a landing place—Ararat and Mount Nisir.
8. Both include striking details, such as sending out the dove and raven.
9. Both describe acts of worship as the passengers emerge from the ark.
10. Both allude to the blessings then bestowed upon them.[6]

Through the years, many additional flood accounts have been found, representing practically all of the great civilizations of antiquity. The flood story was well known and very popular. As Unger states: "The deluge was remembered as a great crisis in human history and preserved through oral tradition and upon cuneiform tablet."[7]

These secular accounts of a flood are one evidence that the great Flood of the Bible actually occurred. The Babylonian accounts, however, like that of creation, are sad distortions involving selfish and angry gods. By the time they were recorded, the great apostasy had set in and the true God had been rejected. Earth's inhabitants had become polytheists, worshiping the creatures rather than the Creator.

The Sumerian King List and earth's first city

Among the finds at Nippur, one of the most significant was that of the Sumerian King List, dating to about 2000 B.C. This remarkable list goes back to the very beginning of presently known recorded civilization. The fascinating text begins: "When kingship was lowered from heaven the kingship was in Eridu."[8]

Eridu could be the sight of the biblical Garden of Eden. The ancient city stood just a few miles south of Ur, near the Persian Gulf. Tablets from that region speak of a garden in which there was a sacred tree. The second chapter of Genesis states that the garden was watered by four rivers, two of which were the Tigris and the Euphrates.

This amazing Sumerian King List has a direct relationship to the biblical record. It lists eight kings who reigned before the Flood. Scholars have questioned the long reigns of the antediluvian kings of the Bible. But the average reign of a king on the Sumerian King List is forty thousand years. And what is equally significant is that in both the Bible and the king list, the life span following the flood is greatly reduced.

In the king list, the last of the eight kings built the ark. He reigned from Shuruppak, a site that has been excavated. Here, a great flood deposit was found, no doubt the deluge of the Genesis account.

From the text of the Sumerian King List, we read: "After the flood had swept thereover, when the kingship was lowered from heaven the kingship was in Kish."[9]

Excavations at Kish have also revealed a major flood deposit dating to the same period. Twenty-two kings reigned from Kish, then the kingship was transferred to Uruk, the Erech of the Bible, about thirty miles up the valley from Ur. At Erech, archaeologists have found some of the oldest writing, the forerunner of cuneiform. They also found the oldest stone structure known to man—a stone pavement.

The table of the nations

Genesis 10 gives us the table of the nations following the Flood. Verse 1 reads: "Now these are the generations of the sons of Noah, Shem, Ham, and Japheth: and unto them were sons born after the flood."

Japheth's descendants were the Indo-Europeans, including the Greeks.

The sons of Ham inhabited North Africa and Canaan and

moved northward and eastward into Mesopotamia. One of Ham's sons was Cush, who gave birth to Nimrod. Of Nimrod we read: "The beginning of his kingdom was Babel, and Erech, and Accad, and Calneh, in the land of Shinar [Sumer]" (Genesis 10:10).

It is significant, and more than coincidental, that the names of these oldest cities after the Flood are the same as those appearing in the early Sumerian texts. The Genesis account continues, "Out of that land went forth Asshur, and builded Nineveh, and the city Rehoboth, and Calah" (Genesis 10:11).

Excavations at both Nineveh and Calah confirm that these cities were seats of the earliest civilizations, along with Babel, Erech, and Accad. This, too, is more than coincidence. So we see again how archaeology confirms the historical reliability of the Bible even in the earliest ancient times.

One of the greatest of the ancient rulers was Sargon the Great, who became king of the city of Akkad. As a result, his people came to be known as Akkadians. About 2400 B.C., he conquered old Babylonia and moved westward as far as the Mediterranean Sea. He became the most powerful monarch who had ever ruled in Mesopotamia. His daughter was installed at Ur as high-priestess of Nannar, the moon god. Some Bible scholars believe Sargon is the mighty Nimrod of the Bible, who established the civilization that eventually erected the Tower of Babel in defiance of the true God.

The Tower of Babel

Archaeologists have made some remarkable discoveries that shed light on the biblical account of the Tower of Babel. In 1952, Dr. Samuel Kramer, while studying some ancient Sumerian clay tablets in the University of Pennsylvania museum, came across an interesting poem describing Sumer's "golden age."

136. Once upon a time there was no snake, there was no scorpion,

> There was no hyena, there was no lion,
> There was no wild(?) dog, no wolf,
> There was no fear, no terror,
> 140. Man had no rival.
> In those days, the lands Subur (and) Hamazi,
> Harmony-tongued(?) Sumer, the great land of the decrees of princeship,
> Uri, the land having all that is appropriate (?),
> The land Martu, resting in security,
> 145. The whole universe, the people in unison(?),
> To Enlil in one tongue. . . .
> Then a-da the lord, a-da the prince, a-da the king,
> Enki a-da the lord, a-da the prince, a-da the king,
> a-da the lord, a-da the prince, a-da the king.[10]

The first eleven lines portray a period when people, free from fear, lived in a world of peace and prosperity. Line 146 contains the phrase "in one tongue," but the verb is missing. It could mean that all peoples spoke the same language, or it could be a figurative expression meaning that all people were "of one heart" in their worship of Enlil. Also, the last part of the poem was missing.

The tantalizing riddle was solved fifteen years later when another tablet bearing the same poem came to light. Not only does it contain the missing verb (which turned out to be *spoke*), but it also contains the last six lines of the poem that were missing in the earlier tablet.

> 150. Enki, the lord of abundance, [whose] commands are trustworthy
> The lord of wisdom, who understands the land,
> The leader of the gods,
> Endowed with wisdom, the l[ord] of Eridu,
> Changed the speech in their mouths, [brought(?)] contention into it,
> Into the speech of man that [until then] had been one.[11]

As Kramer explains, this "puts it beyond all doubt that the Sumerians believed that there was a time when all mankind spoke one and the same language." Also, that the " 'confounding' of tongues came about as the result of rivalry."

The message from the Sumerian tablets is remarkably similar to the Genesis account. There we read:

> And the whole earth was of one language, and of one speech. And it came to pass, as they journeyed from the east, that they found a plain in the land of Shinar [Sumer]; and they dwelt there. And they said one to another, Go to, let us make brick, and burn them throughly. And they had brick for stone, and slime had they for morter. And they said, Go to, let us build us a city and a tower, whose top may reach unto heaven; and let us make us a name, lest we be scattered abroad upon the face of the whole earth. And the Lord came down to see the city and the tower, which the children of men builded. And the Lord said, Behold, the people is one, and they have all one language; and this they begin to do: and now nothing will be restrained from them, which they have imagined to do. Go to, let us go down, and there confound their language, that they may not understand one another's speech. So the Lord scattered them abroad from thence upon the face of all the earth: and they left off to build the city. Therefore is the name of it called Babel (Genesis 11:1-9).

Comparing the tablets from Nippur with the Genesis account reveals a striking similarity. In both accounts people enjoy universal peace and a single language. Then the language is changed, and more than one language is spoken.

The biblical record of the confusion of languages when the Tower of Babel was built happened during the third millennium B.C.; according to Ussher's chronology, about 2234 B.C.

From Nippur, Babylon, Ur, and other ancient cities of that

time come parallel records of the Tower of Babel, written on clay.

Towers, or ziggurats, as they are called, became common to Mesopotamia, and the one at Babylon was the grandfather of them all. Nothing except its foundation and part of its core remains, but excavations confirm its great antiquity.

Ziggurat means "hill of heaven." It is clear that after the Flood people did build "high towers to heaven." All together, about two dozen ziggurats have been found in the land of ancient Sumer. One of the best-preserved ziggurats dominates the landscape of Ur, the home of Abraham, where vast excavations have been carried forward with fantastic, almost unbelievable results. So that is where we will look next.

---

1. C. W. Ceram, *Gods, Graves, and Scholars* (Alfred A. Knopf, 1951), 272.

2. Merrill F. Unger, *Archaeology and the Old Testament* (Grand Rapids, Mich.: Zondervan, 1954), 37.

3. James B. Pritchard, *The Ancient Near East—an Anthology of Texts and Pictures* (Princeton, N.J.: Princeton University Press, 1958), 69, 70, Tablet XI, lines 138-148.

4. Ibid., 66-70, lines 24-27, 84-86, 91-93, 113-115, 132, 133, 155, 156.

5. Jack Finegan, *Light From the Ancient Past* (Princeton, N.J.: Princeton University Press, 1946), 27.

6. Adapted from Unger, *Archaeology and the Old Testament*, 55-65.

7. Ibid., 47.

8. Finegan, *Light From the Ancient Past*, 24.

9. Ibid., 26.

10. Samuel Noah Kramer, "The 'Babel of Tongues': A Sumerian Version," *Journal of the American Oriental Society*, vol. 88 (1968), 109.

11. Ibid., 111.

Chapter 3

The Amazing Finds at Ur and Ebla

Those visiting Ur of the Chaldees, now a vast, desolate place, find it difficult to imagine that they are on the site of what was once the bustling, big-city home of Abraham.

Ur is located in the southern reaches of Mesopotamia, two hundred miles southeast of Baghdad in present-day Iraq. Today we walk over drab clay and scorching sand, but four thousand years ago Ur was the capital city of a prosperous and flourishing civilization.

As we look about, there is ample evidence that the archaeologists have been at work. The excavations were primarily the work of Leonard Woolley, who dug here from 1922 to 1934 under the direction of the British Museum in London and the University Museum of the University of Pennsylvania. The amazing results have so revolutionized our concept of the days of Abraham that Bible scholars have had to rewrite their manuscripts relating to the patriarchal age.[1]

Excavations at Ur

At Ur, Woolley uncovered one of the most unusual cemeteries ever to be found. It was actually one cemetery above another, a whole series of them, covering hundreds of years and dating back into the Sumerian civilization of the third millennium B.C.

The workmen came across a huge pit of graves, two hundred feet across and thirty to forty feet deep. Digging deeper, they found an eight-foot layer of clean clay, obviously laid down by water. Woolley wrote extensively about it. He reported a distinct break between the civilization above and below the flood level. Although not to be identified with the universal Flood of the Bible, it must have been a major deluge that affected all of that society.

The royal graves

Of special interest were the royal graves, huge underground buildings, usually with four rooms. No two buildings were alike. Each grave was beneath later graves.

Coming across a huge ramp, Woolley dug deeper and deeper. Suddenly five bodies were found, then more, and still more. Also, along the ramp they found a lyre, or harp, decorated with an ornamental bronze head of a bull, the Sumerian symbol of fertility.

The ramp led down to a huge burial pit. Just inside the pit stood a wooden chariot built as a sled. Close to the chariot lay a gaming board, artistically decorated with magnificent inlay.

The great pit proved to be a most unusual cemetery, with bodies laid out neatly, side by side, with no sign of any struggle. Evidently these attendants had laid down their lives voluntarily so they could continue their service to the king in the afterlife.

There was still no sign of the king's chamber, just that of the servants. Continuing the dig, Woolley found another ramp, lined with more bodies. This ramp led to a large stone chamber—the royal tomb!

Here they found two four-wheeled wooden wagons drawn by oxen. The sides of the stone chamber were lined with the bodies of soldiers carrying daggers, along with some women. All had been a part of the king's retinue, and all had apparently laid down their lives willingly. It must have been considered a great honor to be buried with their king and, thus, continue their service beyond the grave.

Several skulls, adorned with fancy headdresses of fine jewelry, were recovered and present an unusual exhibit in the University of Pennsylvania museum.

All together, four harps were found. The king must have had his harpist, like David some fifteen hundred years later.

The king's chamber had been looted, but the queen's chamber below was untouched. Her fancy headdress is displayed in the university museum, along with other treasures, including her lyre. Equally fascinating displays from Ur may also be seen in the British Museum and the archaeological museum in Baghdad.

The burial pits were of tremendous proportions. In one of them, sixty-two servants and soldiers were buried with the king and twenty-five with the queen. The largest death pit measured thirty-seven by twenty-four feet. In it, they found sixty men servants and sixty-eight women servants, all laid out neatly in rows, lying on their sides with legs slightly bent. The women wore ribbons of gold and silver, although the silver had disintegrated. Great gold earrings were still in place. Other articles included golden cups, daggers, and helmets—often fashioned from a single piece of gold.

Searching through the treasures of the largest of the royal tombs, Woolley's team came across two magnificent panels, each measuring twenty-two inches long and nine inches high. They represented fantastic skill in metalwork. They were found lying next to the shoulders of a man who may have been their standard bearer.

Among the most unique objects to come from the Ur death pits, and now displayed in the University of Pennsylvania museum, is a statue of a ram caught in a thicket. Although reminiscent of Abraham's experience on Mount Moriah with his son Isaac, this object dates back several hundred years before Abraham was born.

Man's earliest civilization was once identified with Egypt.

Now it is known that Egypt borrowed some aspects of its civilization from the Sumerians of Mesopotamia, as is shown by the excavations at Ur. The wisdom of the Sumerians, the world's earliest civilization, was passed on to the great empires of Egypt, Assyria, and Babylon—and on to the Hebrews, Phoenicians, and Greeks. As one historian puts it, they were the pioneers of the progress of Western man.

Excavations at Ur confirm the Bible

The Sumerian King List, mentioned earlier, was found at Nippur. This remarkable list gives us the names of the kings and dynasties that reigned before and after the Flood. The third dynasty after the Flood is called the first dynasty of Ur.

For many years these early dynasties were regarded by scholars as mythical—just legend, or the result of someone's imagination. But the discoveries at Ur have helped to correct this misconception.

According to the Sumerian King List, the first dynasty of Ur was founded by a king with the long name Mes-anni-padda. He supposedly lived for eighty years, but few believed that he had actually lived at all. Then one day a workman handed Woolley a small tablet of white limestone. The inscription read: "A-anni-pad-da king of Ur, son of Mes-anni-pad-da king of Ur, has built this for his Lady Nin-kharsag."[2]

The tablet had been laid as the foundation stone of the building. Woolley considered this small find the most important of all his discoveries at Ur, for it proved the historical reliability of the Sumerian King List.

A number of important temples were uncovered at Ur. For centuries this great city must have been an important religious center. The University of Pennsylvania museum displays a portion of the mosaic frieze from the temple of Al 'Ubaid, a site near Ur. In the temple and in the graves of this area were relics dating back to the time of Sargon the Great, possibly the great Nimrod of the book of Genesis (see Genesis 10:8).

Scholars had questioned Sargon's existence—he was just another mythical character, they thought. Now, much is known about him and his household. Within the temple, cylinder seals of Sargon's wife's hairdresser were discovered, and seals of her scribe and the steward of the household of Sargon's daughter.

Another prize find was the victory stele of Sargon I's grandson, Naram-Sin. He had restored the empire of Sargon after it had been weakened by Sargon's two sons. A master-piece of Mesopotamian art, the stele was found by the French at Susa and is today one of the important possessions of the Louvre. On it, King Naram-Sin, followed by his soldiers, is seen climbing a steep mountain and treading upon the corpses of his enemies.

Following the death of Naram-Sin, mountain nomads swept through the land and ruled for almost a century, adopting the Sumerian-Akkadian culture. They were followed by the rulers of Lagash, Gudea being their most famous and greatest king. Several of his statues, now in the Louvre, were found by the French.

King Gudea built temples, expanded commercial relations, and made remarkable contributions to literature. During the Lagash period, Sumerian culture enjoyed a renaissance that is reminiscent of the days before they were conquered by Sargon, the Akkadian king.

The mystery of Ebla

In the literature of Ur, mention is made of commercial relations with Ebla. Sargon's grandson, Naram-Sin, had styled himself "conqueror of Arman and Ebla."

Later tablets from Ur, during the period of Abraham (about 2000 B.C.), made frequent mention of Ebla. The texts mention the Eblaites visiting Sumer. Evidently the nation of the Eblaites had existed for a long time, and it had exerted a remarkably important influence. But where was her capital city? Was it Ebla? If so, where was Ebla? And over what area had the Eblaites ruled? Here was a mystery waiting to be solved.

In 1964, a twenty-four-year-old Italian archaeologist, Paolo Matthiae, began digging at a mound in Syria known as Tell Mardikh, forty-three miles south of Aleppo. With his crew, he dug year after year with some small results, but with no texts or identification of the city. Then, after five years of effort, they uncovered a headless statue. An inscription identified it as the king of Ebla.

Now, with great anticipation, they dug on. But five more difficult years dragged on. Then suddenly, they came upon a horde of forty-two cuneiform tablets. Excited at the discovery, Matthiae summoned his epigrapher, Giovanni Pettinato, to come to examine the tablets. Pettinato could read the characters, but they did not make sense in the Sumerian language. Pettinato took the hand copies of the tablets back to Rome for further study. There he was able to decipher them as written in a very early form of the Canaanite language.

Hopes were raised that they might have found the capital city of Ebla. Three months later, a library of one thousand tablets was discovered. Now they were certain. They had indeed been excavating ancient Ebla.

But more was to come. Three months later, a great library of fifteen thousand tablets and fragments of tablets was uncovered. This was more than they could ever have dreamed of—the greatest discovery since that of the Dead Sea Scrolls in 1947.

In 1976, the amazing story hit the news media. And that year, still more tablets were found. By 1978, the number of tablets and fragments had grown to twenty thousand. After fourteen years of excavations, Dr. Matthiae's dig had paid off very well.

According to these excavations, the royal palace had been destroyed by fire back in the third millennium B.C. And that might be considered an act of providence. The tablets were originally of sunbaked brick that under normal conditions would have perished centuries before. But now they were oven-baked and, therefore, well preserved.

Ebla, capital of Syria

In May 1980, the author listened to Dr. Pettinato lecture on the Ebla tablets in Washington, D.C. Pettinato's first official report, *The Archives of Ebla*, was published in late 1981.[3]

The messages from the Ebla tablets have produced more information relating to this ancient period than all previous records and inscriptions combined. They brought to light a vast Syrian Empire that dominated much of the world in the third millennium B.C., competing with the Sumerian civilization to the east.

Before this discovery, Syria in that ancient period was an unknown region between Egypt and Mesopotamia, almost a blank. Now she suddenly emerges as a dominant power over this whole area, with Ebla as her capital. Not only has Ebla been uncovered, but her library of tablets has brought to light a new dimension to the whole world of the ancient Near East by revealing Ebla's relationships with other nations.

When Ebla came to power, Khufu was building one of the Great Pyramids of Egypt. In Mesopotamia, the Land of Sumer was being governed from Kish. Ebla was once strong enough to threaten Sumer. But one of the Sumerian kings of Kish fought and defeated Ebla, and he was known for generations after as "the destroyer of Ebla."

Ebla, Lagash, and Mari

As stated previously, the city-state of Lagash later ruled over Sumer. King Gudea of the Second Dynasty of Lagash (2150-2110 B.C.) mentions commercial relations with the Eblaites of Syria.

Also important to this period was Mari, the capital of another city-state. Excavations at Mari show that she exerted considerable influence until she was finally defeated and destroyed by the powerful Hammurabi, about 1700 B.C.

The Ebla tablets mention Mari some five hundred times. They speak of a time when Mari was badly defeated in battle and forced to pay heavy tribute in gold and silver. One of the tablets lists seventeen countries that were subject to Ebla.

An ancient economic colossus

The majority of the Ebla tablets were of an economic or administrative nature. Commerce was Ebla's chief activity. It was, in fact, what Pettinato calls an economic-commercial colossus, with all of the records of its many activities carefully kept.

Ebla manufactured many goods and exported them far and wide, chief among which were fabrics. All together she produced a thousand varieties, including "damask," which is a fabric intertwined with golden thread. It is believed that it was from this fabric that Syria's greatest city, Damascus, received its name. And in Damascus today, the world-famous textile industry continues, as a visit to its equally famous bazaars makes very evident. It is believed that some of the techniques still used in Damascus may have had their origin at Ebla.

The Ebla tablets speak often of her impressive metal business. Gold was crafted and exported. The purity of the gold was always indicated, similar to the way the term *carat* is used today. Silver was most common, with tons of it on hand. Much of Ebla's gold and silver must have come in as tribute from the many countries that she dominated.

Ebla operated what must have been a very famous scribal school, for students came from all over the empire to learn the skills of writing. Among the first tablets found at Ebla were exercise tablets. The many fascinating tablets give interesting details on how the schools were conducted. The names of the examining professors are given, evidence of scholastic advancement is recorded, and the rank of a professor is always given with a signature, like our degrees today. Pettinato was able to trace the advancement of one student from a "scribe" to a "teacher" and finally to a top "administrator."

Some tablets were like textbooks, serving as the basis for their lessons. Some tablets parsed verbs (for example: "I have given," "he has given," "he has not given," "he may be given"). Other tablets contained dictionaries and vocabularies, some with up to three thousand words, all arranged according to their first elements, like our alphabet.

There were also encyclopedias arranged by subjects. These reveal a remarkable knowledge of botany, zoology, mineralogy, and more. There were lists of birds, animals, fish, precious stones, plants, and trees. One tablet lists 142 birds.

There were also lists of proper names and of professions. It is obvious that ancient peoples had a high degree of intelligence, a fact that comes through loud and clear in the clay tablets of Ebla. Humanity's course has been downward, not upward as proposed by the theory of evolution.

The Ebla tablets vindicate the Bible

The literary texts are of special interest. The library at Ebla contained two copies of the famous Gilgamesh Epic, plus twenty myths and a number of religious texts. As we have come to expect, many of these have a direct relationship to the Bible. This includes an account of creation that has the heaven, earth, sun, and moon appearing in the same order as in Genesis 1. It reads in part:

Lord of heaven and earth:
the earth was not, you created it,
The light of the day was not, you created it.
The morning light you had not [yet] made exist.[4]

The Ebla tablets contained the names of many of the cities and persons mentioned in the Old Testament Scriptures, some of which had never before appeared outside the Bible. Significant among them were the names of Sodom and Gomorrah, as well as Zoar. The names of persons included

Adam, Israel, Saul, and David, showing that such names were common in Bible times.

The discoveries of Ebla came at a time when the higher criticism advocates were reasserting their doubts regarding the historical accuracy of the patriarchal stories. Again the biblical account has been vindicated, and in a most sensational manner.

1. The primary source for this chapter is the work of Sir Leonard Woolley, *Ur of the Chaldees* (London: Penguin, 1952).

2. Woolley, *Ur of the Chaldees*, 73.

3. Giovanni Pettinato, *The Archives of Ebla* (New York: Doubleday, 1981).

4. Ibid., 244.

Chapter 4

The Ur of Abraham

Following the days of Gudea of Lagash, we enter the world of Abraham. The period is known as the Dynasty of Ur III, and it existed in the years 2070 to 1960 B.C. Ur-Nammu, the empire builder, established his capital at Ur. Ur was formerly the name of an important city-state, but now it became the capital city of a united Sumerian Empire that dominated Mesopotamia. Ur-Nammu, who reigned sixteen years, was not only a great conqueror, he also became a great ruler, famous for justice and good works.

The ziggurat at Ur

At Ur, Ur-Nammu carried on a massive reconstruction program, practically rebuilding the city. His greatest architectural achievement was the construction of a massive ziggurat, or temple tower—the best preserved of all the ancient towers that once dotted the landscape of Mesopotamia. It stood in a sacred complex, rising to a height of seventy feet.

Several clay cylinders describing the history of the building were found hidden away in the top stage of the tower. These amazing records were not written by Ur-Nammu, but by Nabonidus, who lived fifteen hundred years later. He was the last ruler of Babylon, reigning jointly with his son Belshazzar at the time of its fall.

The cylinders tell a fascinating story. The tower was founded by Ur-Nammu, but Ur-Nammu died before he could complete its construction. So his son, Sulgi, completed the project. The tower gradually deteriorated during the fifteen long centuries until Nabonidus came along. On the cylinder he tells how he restored the tower.

The ziggurat was originally built in four stages with a shrine at the top dedicated to Nannar, the moon god, chief god of Ur. The University of Pennsylvania museum displays some of the beautifully glazed bricks that once formed a part of the shrine that crowned the top.

A prize possession of the museum is some panels of a huge monument that stood approximately fifteen feet high and five feet wide. Woolley's workmen came across it while clearing the ground fronting the sanctuary that faced the ziggurat.[1]

Monuments of this nature are usually of war scenes, but only the top panel of this monument is a war scene. It depicts King Ur-Nammu seated upon his throne while prisoners with bound hands are led to him. Two panels show Ur-Nammu sacrificing to the gods. Two panels show him standing in an attitude of prayer while a flying god, or genie, pours water from a vase onto the ground. The king thus assigns credit to his god for supplying life-giving water.

Three panels relate to the construction of the tower. First, Ur-Nammu is shown making libations to the god Nannar. Then, on the opposite side of the stele, he is making libations to the wife of Nannar, also a goddess. In the third panel, Nannar holds out the measuring rod and coiled line of the architect, thus symbolizing Nannar's call to the king to build him a house.

In the next scene, which is incomplete, the king presents himself to Nannar, bearing on his shoulder the tools of a builder—compasses, mortar-basket, pick, and shovel.

The lower panel is still more fragmentary. In it, workmen are seen carrying mortar up a ladder and laying the bricks of the tower.

A look at the tower itself reveals that the wall slopes slightly inward. Also, the wall from the top to the bottom is slightly convex, creating an optical illusion. The tower is a masterpiece of construction, so designed that the eye is naturally directed to the shrine at the top, the tower's focal point. The builders of the great Parthenon at Athens had nothing over the builders of Ur some sixteen hundred years earlier, almost a hundred years before the birth of Abraham.

One stands amazed at the marvelous preservation of the bricks. The core is all of sun-dried brick, while the facing was of burnt brick, with the name of Nabonidus stamped on them.

At Ur, one may observe the reconstruction of recent years. The tower is approached by three giant staircases, each with one hundred steps, all of which have been restored, along with some of the massive walls that enclose the sacred complex.

The lower stage was originally black, representing the earth and the dark underworld. The upper stage was red, representing the heavens and the sun. The shrine crowning the top was of blue glazed tile.

The name *ziggurat* means "pinnacle," or "mountaintop." Like the original Tower of Babel, all succeeding ones were designed as staircases to heaven.

Woolley noticed that the tower had periodic tall, narrow slits that were obviously for draining water. But why, he wondered, would they be necessary in a land where rain falls so infrequently? The answer came in an inscription on which Nabonidus explains that the terraces were covered with soil, and trees were planted there—just like the hanging gardens of Nebuchadnezzar's Babylon. The slits were for draining off the irrigation water.

Within the sacred complex were several temples. An inscription found within one of them reads: "'Bur-Sin king of Ur, King of Sumer and Akkad, king of the Four Quarters of the Earth, has built this to his lady Nin-Gal.' "[2]

The University of Pennsylvania museum displays a model, or reconstruction, of one of the small temples. The temples were veritable museums with all sorts of treasures donated by pious kings and others. Brick boxes found under the floor of one temple were filled with a variety of clay figurine gods—in the form of snakes, dogs, human figures, and men with heads of lions and bulls. The gods were believed to guard the house and keep off sickness and bad luck. The cuneiform texts give us many of their prayers and incantations.

The powerful third Dynasty of Ur came to an end about 1960 B.C. when the last king of Ur was taken into captivity. Ur continued, however, as an important city under foreign rulers and as a religious center.

About 150 years after Abraham's departure from Ur, Hammurabi incorporated the city into the Babylonian kingdom of the First Dynasty. Ur rebelled during the reign of Samsu-illuna, Hammurabi's son, and he reduced the city to rubble.

Digging up the city of Abraham

Woolley excavated many houses and temples that suffered in the destruction of Ur. The ruins revealed a surprisingly high state of civilization. The people of Abraham's day lived in fancy homes, all built around fancy courts, many of them two stories, some with as many as thirteen or fourteen rooms. The ruins of these houses still stand, some of them up to eighteen feet high.

When, at the call of God, Abraham left Ur, he left a life of comfort and luxury. No longer can he be regarded as an ignorant, wandering desert sheik—as past critics have described him.

Often, private chapels were attached to the homes. In them were niches for the family gods. The gods served as title deeds that determined the inheritance of the property. It was this type of god that Rachel took with her from the household of Laban at Haran (see Genesis 31:30).

Beneath the floors of the homes the excavators found the bodies of the dead, buried where they could continue to inhabit the house.

One of the temples produced a great hoard of tablets on

which were recorded the business carried on in connection with the temple. The gods received tithe, rent, and offerings. Every transaction was recorded on receipts filed in the temple, even if it was for only a single piece of cheese.

Since there were no coins, large storage rooms were necessary. The stores of supplies were for use in the temple. The supplies included sacrificial animals, oil, and materials for making gods. When supplies were drawn, vouchers were issued, giving the name of the recipient and his authority for receiving the goods.

Also on the temple grounds were factories for the manufacture of wood products and for weaving cloth. Elaborate balance sheets were drawn up monthly and quarterly. The names of the workers were listed with a record showing how much wool each received and how much work each did. The cost of producing the product was determined by the value of the food and supplies issued to the worker. From this plush environment, Abraham was called forth to go into an unknown land that God would show him.

Following Abraham's departure and the fall of the powerful Ur III dynasty with the capture of its last king, the land of Sumer and Akkad suffered under the rivalry of competing powers vying for control. The matter was settled two and a half centuries later with the rise to power of Hammurabi of Babylon, who brought the Sumerian era to an end.

During this period, Ur continued to flourish, particularly as a religious center, until she was destroyed by Hammurabi's son.

After the reigns of Hammurabi and his son, Babylon gradually deteriorated under a succession of weak kings and was conquered by the Hittites in 1531 B.C. The Hittites carried away rich booty from Babylon but did not maintain control. Taking advantage of the situation, the Kassites, who had been gradually penetrating the empire, gained control and ruled the former Babylonian Empire for almost four hundred years (ca. 1530-1150 B.C.).

The Kassites ruled from Babylon for the first century or so, then established a secondary capital at Kurigalzu, present-day Aqar Quf, nine miles west of Baghdad. The ancient tower, or ziggurat, of Aqar Quf still stands as a remarkable land-mark that is visible for many miles. In many ways comparable to that of Ur's, the tower has in recent years undergone considerable reconstruction.

Ur reborn

But Ur would rise again. Assyrian and Babylonian kings would later return to restore the city and the temples.

King Nebuchadnezzar restored the whole complex, but it was his stepson Nabonidus who had a special affection for the city and its moon god Nannar. In fact, he alienated himself from the people of the Babylonian Empire by favoring Nannar over Marduk, the chief Babylonian god. For the last ten years of his life, Nabonidus hardly showed up in Babylon. As the ancient inscriptions indicate, he left the rulership of the empire to his son Belshazzar. This accounts for Belshazzar's presence as king of Babylon at the time when the city fell to the Medes and the Persians, as recorded in the fifth chapter of Daniel.

Nabonidus was a pioneer archaeologist. He searched out the full history of Ur. Woolley excavated a museum in Ur that was created by the daughter of Nabonidus, who served as a high priestess in the temple. In the museum were bricks that dated back some twelve hundred years before Nabonidus. The clay label, the earliest museum label known, reads:

"These are copies from bricks found in the ruins of Ur, the work of Bur-Sin king of Ur, which while searching for the ground-plan [of the temple] the Governor of Ur found, and I saw and wrote out for the marvel of behold-ers."[3]

A few years after Nabonidus, the great ziggurat of Ur was

restored by Cyrus, the conqueror of Babylon, the beneficent king who issued the decree that made possible the restoration of the Jewish temple in Jerusalem. In the ruins of the Ur temple, inscribed bricks were found bearing Cyrus's words: "The great gods have delivered all the lands into my hand."[4]

Cyrus was the last name to appear in the ruins of Ur. A few Persian tablets dating to about 450 B.C. were found, but after that there is nothing.

The Persians adopted the religion of Zoroastrianism, a creed that had no use for images and temples, so decay set in. And Bedouins pitched their tents in the shadow of Ur's ziggurat, which they called "the mound of pitch." They may not even have realized that Abraham, the father of their race, once lived there.

---

1. Woolley, *Ur of the Chaldees*, 100-102.
2. Ibid., 118.
3. Ibid., 157.
4. Ibid., 158.

Chapter 5

From Ur
to Canaan

L eaving behind a life of comfort and luxury, Abraham heard the call of God and obeyed. "By faith Abraham, when he was called to go out into a place which he should after receive for an inheritance, obeyed; and he went out, not knowing whither he went" (Hebrews 11:8).

Together with his father and family, Abraham first journeyed to Haran, a distance of some 550 miles, about halfway to Canaan. For most of the way, they would have followed the course of the Euphrates River.

Cities through which they passed would have included Nippur, Kish, Babylon, and Mari. Mari was then the capital of a city-state reaching from Babylon to Carchemish, 70 miles beyond Haran. She was, in fact, one of the greatest cities of the day and an important stop on the trade route between the Persian Gulf and the Mediterranean. One of the clay tablets from Ugarit, on the Syrian coast, has a citizen boasting, "I have been to Mari." When Abraham's family passed by, Mari would have been at the peak of her activity.

In 1933, a family in that area, while digging a grave for a relative who had died, came across a stone corpse that proved to be that of the king of Mari. Excavations have been conducted there almost continuously by the French since 1933, with amazing results.

A number of temples were uncovered, but more important

was the discovery of the king's palace, the largest and most complete ancient palace ever found. It predated the late Assyrian period of the ninth century B.C. The palatial estate covered over fifteen acres and had close to three hundred rooms, many of them adorned with beautiful mural paintings. One of special interest is now in the Louvre in Paris. The scene is very similar to the biblical story of the Garden of Eden.

An even more important discovery was the library found within the palace—an amazing collection of more than twenty thousand cuneiform clay tablets. The Mari tablets have done much to illuminate the age of Abraham and the patriarchs, offering many parallels to the background and customs of the Old Testament. Interestingly, among cities mentioned in the tablets are Nahor and Haran.

Mari was destroyed by the great Hammurabi of Babylon about 1760 B.C., almost 250 years after Abraham passed through her borders.

From Mari, Abraham's caravan continued on up the Euphrates for another 150 miles or so and then turned northward up the Balikh river to Haran, another fifty miles.

Haran—then and now

When I visited Haran in 1975, we traveled past the present city of Urfa, a few miles before the Haran turnoff. A city of about forty thousand persons, Urfa—with a massive crusader castle crowning its height—featured prominently during the Christian Crusades. The entire area, including Haran, was held by the crusaders for some 150 years.

The tradition of Abraham still persists in the area. Present-day Muslims, especially at Urfa and nearby Ain el-Khalil, still recount legends about the great patriarch, whom they consider to be an Islamic saint.[*]

Leaving the main highway, a battered yellow road sign informed us, "Haran 12 km." Traveling on, we detected a distant tell, or mound, then another, and also a third. It hardly seemed possible that each mound enclosed a long-lost city, or series of cities, one above the other.

It is significant that several of the cities of the area were given the names of Abraham's family members. According to the Bible story, following his father's death, Abraham traveled on toward Canaan in company with his nephew Lot, while other family members remained at Haran. It is apparent that Abraham looked on this area as his ancestral home. So the names of Abraham's family members became the names of several of the towns in the area—Peleg, Serug, Nahor, and Terah. To have just one name of a town similar to one of Abraham's relatives might be mere coincidence, but here we have at least four.

Approaching the conspicuous mound of ancient Haran, we met a shepherd returning to his village with a flock of sheep. We naturally thought of Jacob, who spent fourteen years here, caring for the sheep of his uncle Laban to secure Rachel as his bride. On the mound, we approached a most unusual village, dotted with row upon row of beehivelike mud dwellings.

The road took us past a huge crusader castle. Haran boasts some of the best-preserved Byzantine and crusader castles in the country. These are grim reminders of the days when the Christian Crusades swept through the area in their efforts to win back the holy places from the Muslims.

As we came to a stop near the central water supply—a lone faucet—two men in flowing Arab dress met us with friendly gestures. A few yards away stood the mud-brick community oven. Soon the village chief appeared, tall, middle-aged, and impressive. In Western dress, except for his Arab headdress, he greeted us in fair English.

After a few pleasantries, he escorted us to his home, a rectangular mud-brick building of two rooms—a kitchen and a living room that were connected to several beehive structures that served as bedrooms for both people and animals. Children played peekaboo from nearby corners, fascinated by the strange visitors, perhaps the first Americans some of the younger ones had ever seen.

We were particularly interested in seeing Abraham's well, a landmark of the area. Yes, the chief would take us there, but not until we sat down for tea. Although we would gladly have forfeited this gift of Arab hospitality, to have done so would have been most offensive. So our party of four, Dr. Walton, Mrs. Doreen Brown, my wife, Olive, and I, squatted down with the chief on the carpeted living-room floor, which was devoid of any furniture.

While sipping the Turkish delicacy ever so gently from small porcelain cups, we wondered where the chief's wife might be. Then, just as we were stepping out of the house, she approached. Quickly putting my camera to my eye, I focused in on what would have made a treasured picture. But it was not to be, for just as quickly the chief pulled the camera from me. "You don't photograph our women."

Finally, we were on our way to Abraham's well in our little rental car, a distance of a mile or two. The road took us past additional ancient remains. The chief described them as "Abraham University."

Abraham's well

We pulled up to Abraham's well, traditionally also identified as the well of Eliezer and Rebekah. As the biblical story goes, Abraham sent his servant, Eliezer, to Haran to get a wife for Isaac. At the well, Eliezer met Rebekah, who had come to draw water. Years later, it was at the well of Haran that Isaac's son, Jacob, met Rachel. It might well have happened where we stood.

Haran figures largely in the story of Abraham and his descendants. Here Abraham secured a wife for his son Isaac. When Jacob fled from Esau, he came here to be with his relatives. Here he married Leah, Rachel, Zilpah, and Bilhah. It was here that all twelve of his sons, except Benjamin, were born. And at Haran, God's special call to Abraham was renewed:

Now the Lord had said unto Abram, Get thee out of thy country, and from thy kindred, and from thy father's house, unto a land that I will shew thee: And I will make of thee a great nation, and I will bless thee, and make thy name great; and thou shalt be a blessing: And I will bless them that bless thee, and curse him that curseth thee: and in thee shall all families of the earth be blessed (Genesis 12:1-3).

God had great plans for Abraham. Through him, all nations were to be blessed. Through him and his posterity the knowledge of the one true God was to be preserved and made known to all the world.

The history of the Old Testament is a history of salvation. The commission given to Abraham was repeated to Isaac, to Jacob, and to Israel as a nation. Israel's history is the story of how they, as God's chosen nation, succeeded or failed to carry out God's plan. The Bible speaks only of those nations that came into contact with Israel or influenced her conduct. Israel's great mission was to reveal the true and living God to the world. Through her line the true Messiah would appear. Israel's mission is the great theme of the Old Testament Scriptures—and it all began with Abraham.

There is no indication of how long Abraham remained in Haran. It must have been several years. But after the death of his father Terah, he, with Lot and his family, "and all their substance," resumed their pilgrimage to the land that God would show them. Their caravan consisted of large herds of cattle, flocks of sheep, and "the souls that they had gotten in Haran" (Genesis 12:5).

Carchemish

The next major city of Abraham's pilgrimage was Carchemish, about seventy miles from Haran. Today, both cities are just inside the Turkish border from Syria. When Abraham passed through, Carchemish was a Hittite bastion.

Later, in Canaan, Abraham would purchase a cave from the Hittites for the burial of his wife (see Genesis 23:19; 25:9).

Excavations at Carchemish have produced extensive Hittite remains. The city was the last Hittite outpost and the last of their cities to be destroyed when the Assyrians brought their civilization to an end in the eighth century B.C.

Scholars once questioned the existence of the Hittites, since there were no records of any such people outside of the Bible; but, as we shall later see, that has changed, and the Bible has been vindicated in a convincing way. Carchemish is mentioned several times in the Bible. One of the references refers to the famous battle fought there between Nebuchadnezzar and the Egyptians in 605 B.C (see Jeremiah 46:2).

Nineveh, capital of the Assyrians, fell to the Babylonians and the Medes in 612 B.C. A remnant fled to Haran, where they were annihilated, bringing the great Assyrian Empire to an end. A few years later, in 605 B.C., Nebuchadnezzar, king of Babylon, defeated Pharaoh Necho of Egypt at Carchemish in one of the decisive battles of history. Among the three great nations vying for control of the world—Assyria, Egypt, and Babylon—Babylon emerged the victor.

About 1,300 years earlier, Abraham, on an equally significant mission, no doubt made his camp within the walls of Carchemish. From Carchemish the patriarch traveled southward along the main caravan route of that day, taking him past Aleppo and into Ebla, which then served as the capital of the great Eblait Empire.

Damascus—garden of the desert

On the fringe of the great Syrian desert at the foot of the Lebanon mountains, Abraham entered the flourishing city of Damascus. Two rivers—the Barada, which flows through the city, and the A'waj—provide ample water, making Damascus a garden spot for travelers over the Fertile Crescent.

Damascus, believed by the Arabs to be the oldest continuously inhabited city in the world, was always the capital of a province or an empire. Today it presents a striking contrast between the old and the new. In the old town, the streets are narrow and lined with miles of covered bazaars that are crowded with donkeys, carts, and pedestrians vying for space. It has always been a manufacturing city, and its various products overflow into the streets.

One of the principal bazaars opens on the Umayyad Mosque, built in A.D. 635, which stands as the greatest monument to the Arab Umayyad Empire. The mosque is reminiscent of the days when Damascus stood as the capital of the Muslim world, before the transfer of the capital to Baghdad.

The famous mosque is decorated with the finest mosaics of colored glass, gold, and mother of pearl. It was built where, about 1000 B.C., a pagan temple had stood and where later the Roman temple to Jupiter once stood. In the late fourth century A.D., Emperor Theodosius destroyed part of the temple and converted it into a church dedicated to John the Baptist, for tradition has it that here the head of the wilderness prophet is buried. A special chapel within the mosque stands over the cave in which John's head is said to be preserved in a golden casket.

The mosque is crowned with a tall minaret known by the Arabs as the "Minaret of Jesus." It is their belief that, at His second coming, Jesus will descend from heaven upon this minaret, there to judge the world and destroy the Antichrist.

Leaving Damascus and continuing southward, the caravan route would have taken Abraham past Hazor, eight miles north of the Sea of Galilee, then across the plain of Megiddo to Shechem. After a long journey, he arrived in Canaan.

---

* Adapted from Finegan, *Light From the Ancient Past*, 56.

Chapter 6

Canaan at Last

Shechem is in the shadow of the mountains named Ebal and Gerizim. In Abraham's day, it was a flourishing and highly fortified city, located in an area that later figured prominently in the history of Israel.

It is not a coincidence that the cities of this early period which are mentioned in the Scriptures are the very cities that archaeology has shown to have existed at that time.

Of the time of Abraham's arrival, the Scripture says, "The Canaanite was then in the land" (Genesis 12:6). Excavations have produced amazing testimony to the Canaanite presence. Huge pagan, open-air sanctuaries with their heathen altars stand exposed at Byblos on the Lebanese coast. A massive Canaanite altar has been uncovered on the tell of Megiddo. Amazing evidence of the depraved moral condition of the Canaanites has come to light at Ras Shamrah, ancient Ugarit, on the north Syrian coast. The Canaanites were a people for whom God's patience had apparently run out.

Conditions in Shechem were much different from those in Haran. There were close ties between Ur and Haran, giving Haran a highly developed civilization. But in Canaan, Abraham was now an alien among foreigners.

At Shechem, God repeated His promise to Abraham, the same promise He had given before he left Ur and Haran, that he and his seed would inherit the land of Canaan. Since he was seventy-five years old and without a child, it took immense faith for Abraham to believe that the Canaanites would be driven out and that the land would belong to him and to his children.

After God promised Abraham that he would inherit the land of Canaan, the Scripture continues, "there builded he an altar unto the Lord, who appeared unto him" (Genesis 12:7). After that, wherever Abraham pitched his tent, he built an altar. By doing so, he bore witness against the idolatry of the Canaanites and testified to his allegiance to the one true God.

On leaving Shechem, Abraham's route took him southward toward Bethel, some twenty miles distant. The road took his caravan through the lightly populated hill country that was then covered with forests. Excavations at Bethel have confirmed that the city existed from the time of the patriarchs.

Here Abraham again built an altar and conducted public worship for his company. As he traveled, the countryside became dotted with the altars of this first great missionary. Wherever he went, he proclaimed the message of the true God.

From Bethel, Abraham's caravan continued south, looking for pasture land. This took them down into the Negev, with Beer-sheba as the principal city. A famine in this region forced them to go down for a time into Egypt.

Parting company with Lot

On their return from Egypt, increased riches in herds and flocks made finding sufficient grazing land increasingly difficult. This led to a quarrel between Abraham's servants and those of his nephew Lot. Abraham magnanimously gave Lot the choice of the best territory—the rich plain of the Jordan River—and he remained in the hill country.

God now spoke to Abraham for the fourth time, re-peating the promise made to him at Ur, Haran, and Shechem:

Lift up now thine eyes, and look from the place where thou art northward, and southward, and eastward, and westward: For all the land which thou seest, to thee will I give it, and to thy seed for ever. . . . Then Abram . . . came and dwelt in the plain of Mamre, which is in Hebron, and built there an altar unto the Lord (Genesis 13:14, 15, 18).

Other translations read "oaks of Mamre" rather than "plain of Mamre."

Abraham was now about twenty miles south of Jerusalem. There, today, tourists are shown what is said to be the very oak under which Abraham rested. However, excavations a few miles away have revealed a settlement from Abraham's time that is more likely the true site.

Bad news

A fugitive, perhaps a servant of Lot, arrived one day with bad news. Chedorlaomer, a great king of the Elamites, and a coalition of three other Babylonian kings had come with their armies and had taken the whole country. They had destroyed the cities and had taken captives, among them Lot, his family, and all his possessions.

They had taken the cities of the plain, the Negev, and had gone as far south as Mt. Seir, or Petra, sixty miles south of the Dead Sea. The Scripture says,

And the vale of Sidim was full of slimepits; and the kings of Sodom and Gomorrah fled. . . . And they took Lot . . . who dwelt in Sodom, and his goods, and departed (Genesis 14:10, 12).

Abraham, with 318 servants, pursued them all the way to Damascus in a great rescue operation.

In the past, this Bible account was regarded by scholars as pure legend. But the names given and the routes pursued all agree exactly with the conditions of that time, as revealed by archaeology, so today the story is generally accepted as being true.

Sodom and Gomorrah, and other cities of the plain, enter

the picture again in Genesis 19. Lot is warned to flee from Sodom, for the city would be destroyed. In the familiar story, his wife turned back and became a pillar of salt. The Scripture says, "The Lord rained upon Sodom and upon Gomorrah brimstone and fire from the Lord out of heaven" (Genesis 19:24).

The New Testament Bible writers accepted this statement as true history. Peter declared,

And turning the cities of Sodom and Gomorrah into ashes condemned them with an overthrow, making them an ensample unto those that after should live ungodly (2 Peter 2:6).

The destruction of these cities became an illustration of the destruction that will come upon this world at the end of time.

What about Sodom and Gomorrah?

The actual existence of Sodom and Gomorrah was often questioned until their names appeared in the Ebla tablets. Their location takes us down to the area of the Dead Sea, the lowest spot on earth, 1,295 feet below sea level. Because it has no outlet, the water there consists of 25 percent salt, and salt deposits cover much of the shoreline. Looking over the area, particularly the southern portion, one sees slime pits, asphalt, and salt pillars, all of which fit exactly into the Genesis description of the area.

The book of Genesis names five cities of the plain. The general belief has been that these cities stood in the southern portion of the Dead Sea, which is now covered with water. But today, those beliefs have changed.

As far back as 1924, Bab edh-Dhra, near the southeastern shore, was identified as an ancient city site, but little attention was given to it for forty years. In 1965, some artifacts appeared that were traced to this area. Bedouins had been excavating there for three years. In 1973, a survey team located four other cities contemporary with Bab edh-Dhra, two of which had definitely been destroyed by fire, and possibly a third.

Two years later major excavations began, sponsored partly by the Smithsonian Museum. Bab edh-Dhra yielded a giant cemetery with three kinds of tombs—shaft tombs, charnel houses, and house tombs.

The shaft tombs of the earliest period consisted of a deep shaft beneath which, usually, five burial chambers would be found. Each chamber contained the bones of about five persons who had been moved from their original graves and brought here.

The charnel, or bone house, tomb was usually rectangular, but sometimes round. One such tomb contained the bones of more than three hundred persons, another more than two hundred. All together, twenty thousand tombs were identified. An estimated five hundred thousand persons had been buried along with three million pottery vessels and thousands of miscellaneous artifacts. Bab edh-Dhra is believed to be Gomorrah.

Since then, even more spectacular results have been uncovered at Numeira, seven miles to the south, which is believed to be Sodom. Here, excavations came up with a layer of ash and debris five feet deep. It could not have been the result of volcanic action, for there are no volcanoes in the area.

Two human skeletons were found in the rubble under a collapsed defense tower. Their death was the result of sudden destruction—much like Pompeii—with no time to flee. This discovery indicates not only the violence, but the surprise with which destruction came upon the city.

There were also signs of an earlier destruction that occurred before the sudden destruction by fire, possibly that caused by the battle of Chedorlaomer.

Surface exploration in the three additional areas led to the conclusion that all five of the cities seem to have been destroyed by fire at about the same time, all of which fits well into the Genesis account.

A son is born

The last seventy-five years of Abraham's life were spent primarily in the Negev in the area of Gerar and Beer-sheba. At Gerar, northwest of Beer-sheba, his son Isaac was finally born. Abraham was one hundred years old and Sarah was ninety. It had been twenty-five years since Abraham first received the promise of a son.

Twice his faith had faltered. Abraham had suggested that Eliezer, their servant, be adopted and become the heir. Then later, Sarah suggested that Abraham take her maidservant, Hagar, and that Hagar's son become his heir. And as a result, Ishmael was born.

Finally, Isaac, the true heir, was born.

Scholars once accepted this entire story as mere legend. But this, too, has changed because of archaeology.

A family was digging a grave in their backyard at Nuzi, near Kirkuk, a number of miles southeast of Nineveh, when they came across some ancient tablets. A major archaeological dig was soon underway, with amazing results. Thousands of inscribed tablets were uncovered, tablets dating back to the period of Abraham and the patriarchs. Almost unbelieving, they found themselves reading about customs exactly the same as those in the Bible story, customs relating to family life, marriage, adoption, the treatment of servants, and laws concerning the birthright.

In regard to adoption, a childless couple could adopt a servant to become the heir. However, if a child should later be born, the adopted son must yield.

In regard to marriage, if a wife were barren, she must furnish her husband with a slave wife.

The actions of Abraham and Sarah in the twentieth or nineteenth century B.C. were in complete harmony with the customs of their time. But they would have been out of place if the events had occurred in the ninth or eighth century B.C., when, critics once contended, these narratives were written down.

Though Abraham's faith had not been perfect, he passed the supreme and final test. He was willing to offer his only son Isaac, the heir of the promise, as a sacrifice, for he believed God would raise Isaac from the dead (see Hebrews 11:19).

At Beer-sheba, Abraham lived out most of his later years. The traditional well of Abraham may still be seen today. The remains of the ancient city probably rest beneath the present city and cannot be excavated. However, an excavated tell about four miles from the present Beer-sheba gave evidence of occupation during the period of the Hebrew kings.

When Sarah died, Abraham purchased the cave of Machpelah in Hebron from the Hittites as a burial place for her. One of Islam's most sacred mosques stands over the ancient site. Later, Abraham was also buried in the cave of Machpelah, as were Isaac and Rebekah, and Jacob and Leah.

Abraham died without inheriting the promised land of Canaan, but his faith reached beyond the tomb. He looked beyond this life to the eternal inheritance of all the saved—the heavenly Canaan Hebrews (see 11:10, 13, 16).

Chapter 7

From Canaan to Egypt

T he Negev desert, so familiar to Abraham, also figured prominently in the lives of his son Isaac and his grandson Jacob—whose name God changed to Israel. Israel's children wandered many years in the Negev after they left Egypt, before entering the Promised Land.

Light from Nuzi

Thanks to the amazing tablets discovered at Nuzi, we can now read the biblical account of Abraham and his descendants with new confidence and insight.

The Bible states that Esau sold his birthright to Jacob for a pot of porridge. Such a transfer of birthright was perfectly legal. One of the Nuzi tablets tells how a birthright was sold for three sheep.

Before his death, Jacob gathered his sons about him and pronounced his blessing upon them. And according to the Nuzi law, oral blessings were binding in court.

Harvard University, among others, sponsored a dig at Nuzi. When I visited the university museum, Dr. E. C. Gavin, the chief assistant to the curator, opened clusters of drawers filled with tablets from Nuzi. Then he pointed to huge wooden boxes packed with more tablets. "These are all waiting to be read," he said. I wondered what secrets still lay within, what new bit of wisdom might yet break forth to illuminate the pages of Scripture and bring the past to life.

In a classroom, students were reading the Nuzi tablets. Using a magnifying glass, they would transfer the characters from the tablet onto four-by-six cards.

Dr. Gavin drew an object from one of the drawers and handed it to Olive, my wife. He said, "You have now touched a four-thousand-year-old mummified rat."

From Canaan to Egypt's wonders

When Jacob sent his son Joseph in search of his older brothers, Joseph went quite a distance north from Beer-sheba into the central hill country, west of Shechem, to Dothan.

On the beautiful plain before the mound of Dothan there is an ancient well, possibly the very one in which Joseph was placed by his brethren. Later, he was taken from the well and sold as a slave to Midianites on their way to Egypt.

In Egypt, the slave lad was introduced to a civilization that was already the wonder of the world. Memphis, the first capital of the united empire of Egypt, had been one of the world's greatest cities for over five hundred years.

Egypt's history begins at Memphis. Her founder, Menes, is the earliest Egyptian ruler of whom we have any knowledge. With the invasion of the Hyksos about 1720 B.C., the capital was moved north to Avaris in the delta, where it stood in the time of Joseph.

With the expulsion of the Hyksos about 1560 B.C., the capital was transferred to Thebes, about 450 miles south of Memphis to Upper Egypt. Memphis still continued, however, as the capital of Lower Egypt for about another thousand years.

At Memphis today, about twenty miles south of Cairo, there is little to remind us of her former greatness. Among the scattered ruins, however, there stands a colossal sphinx. Sheltered in a museum on the sight is a more colossal statue of Ramses the Great, a later pharaoh of the thirteenth century B.C. A companion to it towers above the Cairo railway station.

Memphis was the headquarters for the worship of Apis, the

sacred bull. Archaeologists have been at work in recent years restoring the Apis Bull Temple.

On higher ground, about three miles above Memphis, lies the earliest royal burial ground of Sakkara. Approaching the site, marked by the great pyramid of Zoser (about 2300 B.C.), I stopped first at the mastaba tomb of Ti, a royal official. The mastaba tombs are the earliest known royal burial chambers. The underground hallways and chambers are adorned with ancient hieroglyphic writing. Inside one of the chambers stands a life-size statue of Ti himself.

The mastaba tombs were originally covered with large superstructures. The structure over the tomb of Ti contained twenty-seven cells or storage rooms for articles that would be needed in the afterlife. Beneath, a deep shaft led down to the burial chamber.

In 1850, Auguste Mariette of the Louvre in Paris was walking over the area toward the Zoser pyramid when he discovered a sphinx head sticking out of the ground. He recalled a statement from Strabo, the Greek geographer, about an avenue of sphinxes leading down to a cemetery of sacred bulls. Could this be it?

It was indeed. Excavations opened up a great ramp lined with sphinxes. It led down to one of the strangest cemeteries in the world, a corridor 1,120 feet long with huge stone coffins on either side. These were the royal burial coffins of the sacred bulls.

A prize bull would be chosen and cared for in the temple at Memphis. At death he would be given a royal burial, and another would be chosen.

Apis bull worship would have been familiar to Joseph. As I walked the length of this great underground chamber, I imagined that he, too, must have visited the strange site.

Statues of the Apis bull adorned Egyptian homes and temples. When Israel at Sinai demanded that Aaron give them a sacred calf to worship, they were but turning back to a form of worship they had practiced in Egypt.

The wonders of the pyramids at Sakkara

Walking through the sand by way of the Sed Temple brought us to the burial ground of Sakkara and the great pyramid of Zoser. All together, Egypt has about eighty pyramids in various stages of preservation. This one, standing higher than a twenty-story building, is the oldest of them all. It was already several centuries old when Abraham, and later Joseph, entered Egypt.

The pyramid stands in a sacred complex once surrounded by a massive wall thirty-three feet high and more than a mile long. Archaeologists, who found it to be one of the richest sites in the world, have been digging there for a hundred years and believe it will take another hundred years to complete their work.

The whole underground is a network of tomb chambers and halls. Zoser's tomb alone consisted of fifty-eight rooms, filled with thousands of articles of pottery and stone.

Not far removed is the pyramid of Una, somewhat less imposing in its present state, but still of major significance. Fronting it is the longest and best preserved of the sacred ways. These streets connected the mortuary temples that fronted the pyramids with their valley temples along the waters of the Nile. Also at Una, portions of the hard granite outer surface that once covered all of the pyramids has been preserved.

A ramp slopes down into the interior of the Una pyramid with its various chambers. On the walls are the best examples of pyramid texts yet found. The texts written by the priests record magical spells that will ensure a pleasant afterlife. To an Egyptian, the pyramids were "stairways to heaven."

The tomb chamber of the Una pyramid still encloses the great stone sarcophagus of the king, but the body has long since been removed and the tomb treasures stolen.

From the heights of the burial grounds of Sakkara, a look south reveals in the distance the second pyramid to be built, the pyramid of Dashur. Slightly bent, it is also called the Bent pyramid.

Farther south is the pyramid of Meidum, the third to be constructed. Following the Meidum pyramid, King Snefru built a second pyramid at Dashur. Snefru was the father of Khufu (2570-2547 B.C.), the builder of the greatest pyramid of all at Giza. He was known by the Greeks as Cheops. Thus we see the transition in so short a time from the first large stone building to the greatest monument in stone ever erected—Khufu's pyramid at Giza.

The greatest pyramid of all

The pyramids of Giza stand on the left bank of the Nile just above Cairo, with Memphis about twenty miles to the south. A visit to Giza is an unforgettable experience.

Both Abraham and Joseph probably visited the great pyramid of King Khufu, for in their time it had been built for several hundred years and must already have been famous as the greatest wonder of the ancient world.

The great stone pyramid of Khufu stands taller than a forty-story building. It was constructed of 2,600,000 blocks of stone averaging two and a half tons each. Cut into one-foot cubes and placed side by side, they would extend two-thirds of the way around the world at the equator.

Just how the pyramids were constructed remains a mystery, although various theories have been advanced. According to Herodotus, the Greek historian, one hundred thousand men worked together in three-month shifts. Ten years were required to build the road up which the stones were dragged and another twenty years to build the pyramid itself. If he is correct, the workmen would have had to lay 315 of these massive stones each day, or 26 an hour, working ten hours a day, six days a week. To have laid just ten of them a day would seem to have been a reasonable number. But then it would have required 664 years to complete the project.

A hike to the top is a breathtaking experience. It is also dangerous—so much so that it is no longer permitted. The top affords an excellent view of the pyramid of Khafre, the second to be built at Giza. Some of the stone outer casing is still intact.

The Khafre pyramid is unique in that it is fronted by the great stone sphinx, 240 feet long, carved out of natural rock. The face is 13 feet, 8 inches across. The nose is 5 feet, 7 inches long and the mouth 7 feet 7 inches wide. It is believed to represent King Khafre as a god standing guard over his own burial site.

There have been many conjectures as to the purpose of the pyramids. Scholars generally agree that they were solely for the burial of the dead. They were "houses of eternity" and stand as man's greatest witness to his early belief in the immortality of the soul.

Near the great pyramid of Khufu is a great pit in which a huge boat was found. Hewed from solid rock, the pit was covered with more than seven hundred tons of limestone blocks. Today the boat may be seen in a large building erected for it at the side of the pyramid. Over 125 feet long, it was the king's own boat and was buried with him so he could continue to have its use in the afterlife. More recently a second boat pit has been discovered near the first. Excavations on it have proceeded since 1983.

To assure continued existence, there were two essentials— the preservation of the king's mortal remains, and arrangements to assure the essentials he would need in the life to come. One essential was the boat that figured so largely in the mortal life of the king and his court.

But as permanent as they have been, the pyramids did not accomplish their purposes. If they were built to protect the burial plots of the kings, they failed. For in every instance, the pyramid tombs have been rifled and the bodies removed.

Chapter 8

The Slave Boy
Makes Good

During the Hyksos' rule, Joseph was sold to the house of Potiphar as a slave. The rulers of Egypt at that time were Asiatics, as was Joseph, which may help to explain the favorable treatment he received. The story of this Hebrew lad and his rise to prominence is one of the most fascinating of all Bible stories. It is also the most lengthy, covering fourteen chapters of the book of Genesis. Like other stories of Genesis, its historical reliability was seriously questioned by the skeptics, who said it was not written until the ninth or eighth century B.C.

Since the decipherment of the ancient hieroglyphic script and language, the skeptics have been proven wrong. For the ancient inscriptions describe conditions, customs, laws, and titles just like those we find in the Bible during this period.

The merchants who carried Joseph down to Egypt sold him for twenty pieces of silver (see Genesis 37:28), the exact price of a slave at that time. Earlier, the price was less, about fifteen pieces—later, it was more.

It is also impressive that the titles given to Egyptian officers were exactly the same as those mentioned in the Bible. Irukkaptah held the office of "Superintendent of the Royal Granary," a position also held by Joseph (see Genesis 41:55-57). Potiphar made Joseph "overseer over his house" (Genesis 39:4), a title corresponding exactly with that of a prime minister. Other official titles appearing both in the Bible and in Egyptian

5—T.I.S.

accounts are "chief butler" and "chief baker" (see Genesis 40:9, 16). The Bible writers used the correct titles for the times, which would not have fit in a later period.

I have watched magicians in Egypt performing their seemingly impossible tricks of magic. Magicians played an important role in ancient times. Dreams were regarded as extremely significant, just as indicated in the Bible account of the dreams of the butler and the baker.

Pharaoh, we are told, placed his signet ring on Joseph's hand. Today such rings dating to his time appear in many museums. The details of the Bible account are correct.

The Genesis account states that Pharaoh also "put a gold chain about [Joseph's] neck." This was also a common practice. The golden necklace worn by King Tutankhamen was among the treasures found in his tomb.

The Scripture says, "He [the king] made him [Joseph] to ride in the second chariot" (Genesis 41:43). The chariot of King Tutankhamen in the Cairo museum is a good example of what such chariots were like.

Embalming, or mummification, was the customary practice at death for persons of importance in Egypt. And the Scripture states that both Jacob and Joseph were embalmed (see Genesis 50:2, 26).

Because of the famine in Canaan, Jacob's sons came down into Egypt to buy grain (see Genesis 42:3). A tomb at Beni Hasan, about 160 miles south of Cairo, contains an instructive painting from the period of the patriarchs showing thirty-seven Palestinians coming into Egypt, reminiscent of the visit by Jacob and his sons.

To view this famous painting, I arranged with a pastor, a native of Cairo, to take me up the Nile. It was a two-day trip of great interest, which included a visit to Tell el-Amarna, of which I will write later. From the small sailing boat in which we crossed the Nile, we could plainly see the tomb openings along the face of the steep eastern cliffs. We landed on the rocky shore at the ruined site of Beni Hasan and took a steep path up to the Egyptian tombs.

Thirty-nine of the tombs represent the Middle Kingdom, the period of the patriarchs. The tombs belonged to the nobles who ruled this Egyptian province almost four thousand years ago. They left colorful murals painted on the walls of the tombs, depicting their life and administration.

The famous painting we were searching for is within the tomb of the noble Khnumhotep . Unfortunately, the painting has faded badly since being exposed to the weather, so it was difficult to make out the scene. However, it was familiar from reproductions of it that I had seen. The thirty-seven people making up the caravan are clearly attired in Asiatic clothing, featuring long cloaks, and they appear carrying spears, bows, and throw sticks. The camel was not yet in general use, so they came with their little donkeys.

The Khnumhotep tomb inscription reads: "The arriving, bringing eye-paint, which thirty-seven Asiatics brought to him."

Evidently, coming into Egypt for barter purposes was common.

The land of Goshen

When his brothers came to buy grain, Joseph invited them to bring their father Jacob to live in Egypt. Jacob and his family settled in the land of Goshen, the most fertile area because it was watered by the tributaries of the Nile. Avaris, near Goshen, was then the capital city.

Avaris is also identified as the site of the city of Rameses. We are told that the Israelite slaves "built for Pharaoh treasure cities, Pithom and Rameses" (Exodus 1:11).

When the Israelites left Egypt, they "removed from Rameses" (Numbers 33:5).

Through the years, Avaris has been identified with Tanis in the eastern Delta, about eighty miles northeast of Cairo. Excavations and research of recent years have cast grave doubts about Tanis being the true site of Avaris and Rameses. The site near Qantir, about fifteen miles south of Tanis, is the more probable location.

At the time of my visit to the tombs of Beni Hasan, I also made a journey northward to explore these areas. Traveling again with the Egyptian pastor, this time accompanied by my wife, I drove along beautiful canals through some of the most fertile areas of Egypt, parts seldom visited by tourists. The road led also through many primitive mud villages. We were fascinated by scenes of men and animals at work in the fields—camels hardly visible beneath heaping loads of alfalfa and oxen going round and round a water pumping station or pulling sleds to thrash out the grain.

Leaving the paved highway, we found the going increasingly rough. At times the road turned out to be no road at all, and we would explore other possibilities, sometimes driving on the banks of canals.

The jostling seemed to tear the car apart, and eventually the muffler did break loose. This meant a stop for repairs at the village of Zoan. The name intrigued us, for Psalm 78:12 and 43 indicate that Zoan witnessed the miracles of Moses.

The supposed eighty miles to Tanis must have been considerably more. But at last the ruins of Tanis appeared, a vast area covering a thousand acres. All together, archaeologists there have uncovered twenty-three fallen obelisks or fragments, and numerous statues and columns. We saw them lying everywhere, most of them made of the hard, rose-red granite found only at Aswan, some seven hundred miles away.

The ruins are almost entirely of the mighty Rameses II (1304-1227 B.C.). A giant statue of him, ninety-two feet tall, once stood here, along with numerous lesser ones. Little wonder scholars believed this to have been the Rameses and Avaris of the Bible, and home to the Israelites.

A problem of identification

But there were problems. Why were there no pottery fragments, scarabs, or inscriptions that dated any of the monuments to the period of Rameses and earlier? According to the existing evidence, this site did not come into existence until the twenty-first dynasty, or about 1100 B.C., 150 years after Rameses had died. The materials for the building and the ornamentation were obviously identified with Rameses, but they had apparently been brought in from another city that had fallen into ruin.

As early as the 1930s, there were those who believed that the fallen city of Rameses was near the present village of Qantir, fifteen miles to the south, a conclusion confirmed by more current diggings. We arrived at Qantir just two days after the Austrian archaeologists under the direction of M. Bietak had completed their season's work. The Institute of Egyptology of the University of Vienna had dug there from 1966 to 1969. The work was resumed in 1975 by the Austrian Archaeological Institute in Cairo. At the headquarters building, we were shown pottery vessels and other objects from the dig.

In 1954, Labib Habachi had carried on extensive work at the same site, uncovering twenty-four palace doorways. The diggings had revealed Tel el-Dabh to be the site of a vast metropolis with massive palaces and temples. This ancient city was laid out in four divisions with a great palace in the center.

The city had flourished as Avaris during the Hyksos period when Joseph and his family were probably in Egypt, but was greatly enlarged and enriched by Rameses the Great. Archaeologist W. C. Hays, among the first to dig there, postulated that the palace in the days of Rameses must have exceeded in grandeur that of any other in Egypt. The palace even included a temple one thousand feet long.

Following the days of Rameses and the Nineteenth Dynasty, the city of Rameses sank into obscurity. During the Twenty-first and Twenty-second Dynasties, around 1100 B.C., the nation of Egypt was in decline, and its wealth was drying up. Its stone walls, monuments, and statues became the quarry for the new capital city at Tanis. As unbelievable as it may appear, the entire city of Avaris/Rameses was quarried away, transported fifteen miles, and the blocks, statues, and monuments erected in their new location at Tanis.

If the identification of Tel el-Dabh as Avaris/Rameses is correct, and the evidence is substantial,* then this was where Joseph would have served in the palace of Pharaoh. Here would have stood the palace of Pharaoh before whom Moses appeared. And from here the Israelites, after the scourge of the plagues, would have begun their Exodus back to the Promised Land (see Exodus 12:37).

Three cities of significance

During the period of Israel's sojourn in Egypt, there were three cities in the Nile Delta of Lower Egypt that had a striking relationship to each other—Qantir, On, and Memphis. Memphis, as noted previously, was the political capital, except during the Hyksos period. On was the religious center, and Qantir the official residence of the pharaohs.

On, also known as Heliopolis, the City of the Sun, is the first city mentioned in the Bible in connection with the Israelites. Genesis 41:45 states that Joseph married the daughter of the priest of On.

Today a lone obelisk, the first to be erected, marks the site of On. It fronted a huge temple dedicated to the sun. On the obelisk is a cartouche, or oblong figure, of King Usertesen, who lived in 2760 B.C.

The kings of Egypt always journeyed to On for their coronation ceremonies and jubilees. On each such occasion, another pair of obelisks would be erected to commemorate the event. But the obelisks have, for the most part, been carted away. To see them today, one must go to Rome, Paris, London, Istanbul, or to Central Park in New York City. The mate to the obelisk in New York is in London. According to Habachi, the two obelisks were originally erected at On by Thutmose III, one of the greatest of Egypt's pharaohs, who died in 1450 B.C. The one in New York stood at the east entrance to the Heliopolis temple, and the one now in London stood on the west.

In New York City, a worthwhile stop is the Brooklyn Museum, where a model of the great Sun Temple of Heliopolis is on display. It is patterned after a model built by Seti I, the father of Rameses II. To the right of this recently constructed model is the actual base of the original model created by the Egyptian pharaoh of the fourteenth century B.C.

The temple at On consisted of two apartments, the holy place and the most holy place—or holy of holies. Within the holy of holies the most sacred object was a pyramid-shaped stone on which it was believed the sun god revealed himself. The great pyramids that emerged in the desert were no doubt patterned after this pyramid-shaped stone at On.

In recent years, the site of the ancient sun temple of On has been developed into a national park and tourist center.

While On was the religious center, Memphis was the political capital and the center of government for eight hundred years. Then came the invasion of the Hyksos, who moved the capital from Memphis to Avaris. When the Hyksos were expelled from Egypt, the capital was moved 450 miles south to Thebes. Memphis, however, regained its position and continued as the northern capital.

The war of liberation from the Hyksos' rule was begun when the local ruler at Thebes, Sekenenre, rebelled. His sons Kamose and Ahmose eventually took the capital at Avaris and drove the Hyksos from Egypt.

Kamose and Ahmose, the liberation kings, left inscriptions in which they boast of their feats of heroism but seldom mention their war against the hated Hyksos, whom they wished to forget. One of Ahmose's captains, however, who rose to the position of naval officer in the Nile fleet of ships, left a record of his battles in the Hyksos war. It is found in a long inscription in his tomb cut into the cliff neighboring his hometown of Nechab, now called Elkab, about fifty miles south of Luxor.

The captain, also bearing the name Ahmose, speaks in considerable detail of his heroic deeds, which included two battles against the Hyksos' capital city of Avaris. In each he acted valiantly, receiving booty and royal decorations.

In a third battle to the south, for which he was again decorated for valor, the Hyksos were again defeated. The city of Avaris was then besieged and taken and the enemy driven from Egypt.

Exodus 1:8 reads: "Now there arose up a new king over Egypt, which knew not Joseph."

The liberators of Egypt who formed the powerful Eighteenth Dynasty were probably the Egyptian kings who "knew not Joseph." Under their rule, Israel was led into slavery, and at their capital city of Thebes there arose the great temples that are today among the world's greatest monuments of ancient civilizations.

---

* For a full treatment of this subject, see *The International Standard Bible Encyclopedia*, s.v. "Exodus, Date of the" (Grand Rapids, Mich.: Eerdmans, 1979). See also Labib Habachi, *The Obelisks of Egypt: Skyscrapers of the Past* (New York: Columbia U. Press, 1985), and Manfred Bietak, "Avaris and Piramesse: Archaeological Exploration in the Eastern Nile Delta," Mortimer Wheeler Archaeological Lecture, 1979.

Chapter 9

The World of Moses

A hmose I, who drove the Hyksos out of Egypt, extended the borders of the empire to the south. He was succeeded by Amenhotep I, who extended the borders still farther south, establishing his capital at the site of the old Seventeenth Dynasty capital at Thebes.

Amenhotep I, the new king, added to the construction of a great temple complex at Thebes erected in the time of the Twelfth Dynasty (2000-1780 B.C.). The temple construction would continue for a thousand years, each new pharaoh adding to it. Dedicated to the god Amon, it became the largest such religious center in the world, the greatest temple ever built by man.

We approached the part of the Amon Temple founded by Amenhotep I by way of the sacred avenue of the sphinxes. We then walked through the first pylon built by Shishak and that of Rameses II, the Great, who ruled Egypt for sixty-seven years. Rameses II added his part to the Amon Temple about 250 years after the part constructed by Amenhotep I, and 165 years after the Exodus. A hike to the top of the pylon of Rameses II offers an unforgettable view of this greatest collection of ancient remains on earth today.

Entering the great enclosure, we passed through the court of Rameses II, which he decorated with various monuments and statues of himself. We passed through additional courts and into the great Hypostyle Hall.

Here the magnificent central columns, eighty-five feet high, towered above us. Atop one of the columns is a single slab of stone large enough for one hundred persons to stand on.

The side aisles of the Hypostyle Hall are a forest of 122 columns, each ten feet in diameter and as high as a four-story building.

Passing through additional courts and chambers, we came to the court of Thutmose I, who succeeded Amenhotep I to the throne during Israel's sojourn in Egypt. History would mark him as the most important king following the expulsion of the Hyksos. With ambitious campaigns, he went about to reestablish the empire.

At Thebes, in the area of present-day Karnak, Thutmose I also erected the first pair of obelisks sixty-five feet tall, one of which remains. Like the many obelisks that would follow, these were made of a single piece of hard granite quarried at Aswan, 150 miles farther up the river and brought to the site on huge barges.

Thutmose I was the first of the pharaohs to record the use of Asiatic slaves in his building operations. This slave labor force would probably have included Israel. While great numbers were engaged in the heavy building activities in the north at Memphis, On, and Avaris, others labored at Thebes in the south.

Thutmose I seems to have been a cruel ruler, hanging the heads of his enemies from his Nile ship and temple walls. Our interest in him increases when we consider that he was perhaps the pharaoh who issued the decree condemning all male slave children to death, including baby Moses.

As the daughter of Thutmose I, Hatshepsut was destined to become one of the most famous women of history. In her palace at Thebes, she reared Moses as an adopted son, perhaps contemplating that some day he would become the king of Egypt.

By another wife, Thutmose I had a son, Thutmose II. Hatshepsut married him, her half brother, and thus became queen. He was sickly and died after a brief reign, and Hatshepsut became pharaoh. Shortly thereafter, Hatshepsut was forced by a revolt of the priests to accept her young nephew and stepson Thutmose III as coregent. Or she may have forced herself upon Thutmose III as coregent. In either event, her actions may have been inspired by her regard for Moses. An inscription on the Amon Temple wall states that Thutmose III came to the throne by the personal intervention of "the god Amon."

During most of this coregency, Hatshepsut managed to keep Thutmose III in the background and ruled the empire in her own right for twenty-two years (1504-1482 B.C.). It must have been during the latter part of this coregency with Thutmose III, when Thutmose III was gaining the upper hand, that Moses was forced to flee to Horeb (Sinai), where he remained for forty years. Shortly after Moses' flight, Hatshepsut disappears from history.

The illustrious Hatshepsut

Consider the illustrious reign of this remarkable woman, the probable stepmother of Moses. At Thebes, she added to the great temple at Karnak, erecting at least four obelisks. One, ninety-seven feet tall, still stands. Its mate is lying on the ground. Inscriptions indicate that to quarry one such obelisk required seven months' work.

Senmut, who supervised the work of building Hatshepsut's temple at Karnak, must have regarded himself as the greatest and wisest man who ever lived. He records:

I was a noble, to whom one hearkened, moreover, I had access to all the writings of the prophets; There was nothing which I did not know of that which had happened since the beginning.[1]

Senmut also supervised the construction of Hatshepsut's fabulous mortuary temple, built against the hills at Deir el-Bahri on the western side of the Nile. The temple rises in impressive terraces that are reached by massive ramps.

Several years ago, a great pit was opened that was filled with broken and mutilated statues of Hatshepsut. These have been restored by the Metropolitan Museum in New York City, where they may be seen today.

How did they get into that pit? Who had them smashed and buried?

Thutmose III, the Napoleon of Egypt

The ancient villain was none other than Hatshepsut's younger stepson, Thutmose III, the son of her half-brother, Thutmose II. As he grew older, he grew sick of playing second fiddle to his stepmother. It appears that he finally had her put out of the way. After her death, he launched a crusade of revenge. Wherever her name appeared, he had it defaced. Her statues were mutilated or destroyed, and a score or more of them were thrown into the great pit.

Destroying her towering obelisk presented a problem. So to hide it, the revengeful pharaoh had a great wall erected all around it. Today a fragment of that wall remains as a monumental reminder of the king's wrath.

Thutmose III became the Napoleon of Egypt. Following the death of Hatshepsut, he expanded the empire to an extent never before reached, conducting military campaigns into Syria-Palestine on an almost annual basis, seventeen in all.

Of particular interest is the graphic account of his most famous battle, one of the famous battles of history—the Battle of Megiddo, fought shortly after the disappearance of Hatshepsut. It is the first battle in history of which we have a detailed account. On the walls of his festival hall the king gives a progress report of each day's march. He recorded where they spent each night and the battle design that won them the victory—all in greatest detail.

Lord Allenby, the great British general, wrote his doctorate on this Battle of Megiddo. Later, during World War I, about 3,500 years after Thutmose's famous victory, Allenby found himself in charge of the allied forces in Palestine. On the same battle ground of Megiddo, using the same battle tactics of Thutmose III, he won an equally decisive victory, earning for himself the title of general. He would ever after be known as "Lord Allenby of Megiddo."

Thutmose III set up at least seven obelisks at Karnak, not one of which remains in Egypt. The seventh stands today outside the church of the Lateran Palace at Rome. It is the tallest ever to be erected, 137 feet high, including the base.

Rome might well be called the "city of obelisks," for she boasts thirteen in all—all from Egypt. Egypt itself is left with only four.

The Lateran obelisk has quite a history. Emperor Augustus had in mind moving it to Rome, but his dream did not come true. Three hundred years later, Constantine removed it from Karnak. He intended to move it to Constantinople, his new capital—the New Rome. But it got only as far as Alexandria, and Constantine died. This delayed the project, and his son had it taken to Rome, where it was set up in the Circus Maximus as a companion to another one already erected there by Augustus.[2]

The obelisk stood for centuries in the Circus Maximus, but then, for reasons that remain a mystery, it fell and was lost. A search in the sixteenth century uncovered it twenty-five feet underground. It was then moved to the Lateran, the official church of the popes, where it stands today. To move it took more than a year. It was dedicated on August 10, 1588.

According to Habachi, the mate to the Lateran obelisk is that which today lies in the quarry at Aswan. It was discarded because of a crack. Without the base, it is 110 feet long and 14 feet across, and weighs 1,168 tons.

The Heliopolis obelisk now standing in New York's Central Park also has a fascinating history. It arrived by ship in New York on July 27, 1880, before a location for it had been determined. Central Park was finally chosen, and on October 9 a grand mason, along with nine thousand other masons and spectators, set the pedestal in place.

With the site selected and the pedestal in place, the 193-ton obelisk was moved through the streets of New York City at a pace of 97 feet a day, making the journey to the site in 112 days. It arrived in Central Park on January 5, 1881, and was raised amid the cheers of ten thousand spectators.[3]

These obelisks of Thutmose III, erected in several places around the world, serve as reminders of the period of Israel's exodus from Egypt.

Who was the pharaoh of the Exodus?

Who was the pharaoh of the Exodus? And when did the Exodus occur? The question has been under dispute for many long years.

A key text of Scripture reads:

It came to pass in the four hundred and eightieth year after the children of Israel were come out of the land of Egypt, in the fourth year of Solomon's reign over Israel . . . that he began to build the house of the Lord (1 Kings 6:1).

Conservative, Bible-believing scholars believe this scripture is the key to determining the date of the Exodus and for identifying the pharaoh of the Exodus. The fourth year of Solomon, the year he began to build the temple, is generally placed at 967/966 B.C. The Israelites would have left Egypt 480 years earlier, or in the spring of 1445 B.C., five years after the death of Thutmose III, and during the reign of Amenhotep II, who succeeded him.[4]

A problem raised is that the pharaoh of the Exodus was supposedly drowned in the Red Sea, whereas Amenhotep II continued to reign for more than twenty additional years.

A revised scenario

William H. Shea suggests a revised scenario along with substantial documentation.[5] Placing the fourth year of

Solomon, the year he began to build the temple, in 971 B.C., Shea arrives at the year 1450 B.C. as the most likely date of the exodus.

According to Shea, Thutmose III, who reigned fifty-four years including his coregency with Hatshepsut, met his death on March 17, 1450 B.C. This would correspond to the time of year that the Passover was instituted on the night of Israel's deliverance and their Exodus from Egypt.

Was Thutmose drowned in the Red Sea? The circumstances of his death are not given. A mummy in the Cairo Museum is said to be that of this king. His age at death would have been at least sixty years. However, the X-rays of this mummy "do not support such an advanced age."[6] According to Shea, the physical anthropologists who have studied the X-rays of this mummy, M. Baer and W. Krogman, estimate his age at death between forty and forty-five years. Since Thutmose III reigned for a minimum of fifty-four years and perhaps more, argues Shea, this mummy could not be Thutmose III, but may be the body of a person substituted for Thutmose after he drowned.

The king who lost his son

Shea advances three lines of evidence revealing, to his satisfaction, that Amenhotep II had reigned as coregent with his father, Thutmose III, for three years at the time of the Exodus.[7] According to Shea, in 1451 B.C., the year before the Exodus, Amenhotep II was sent on an expedition into Syria to quell a rebellion. He returned three months after the Exodus to find both his eldest son and his father, Thutmose III, dead.

This supports the Bible account with Thutmose III as the pharaoh who died in the Red Sea, and Amenhotep II as the pharaoh who lost his firstborn son in the tenth plague.

Continuing Shea's account, Amenhotep II returned home to discover that Egypt's slave labor force had vacated the land and that his father and eldest son were dead. Greatly enraged, he launched a frightful campaign of revenge. At the public "welcome home" function at Memphis, he had seven captive chiefs beheaded and their skulls hung to the bow of his royal boat. The bodies of six of the chiefs were taken to Thebes, where they were hung on the Karnak temple wall. The seventh was taken farther south to Nubia.

Amenhotep II returned to Palestine and Syria in two successive campaigns, returning with ninety thousand captives, no doubt to replenish the slave-labor force depleted by the Exodus of the Israelites.

The inscriptions of Amenhotep's later years reveal an intense hatred for Semites. The last of the texts is so vile, some scholars have concluded that he must have been drunk when he dictated it.

The Shea scenario is a subject of debate among scholars.

The king and his dream

Amenhotep II was succeeded by Thutmose IV, who was not his eldest son and would not normally have assumed the throne. The story of his accession is a fascinating one.

Beneath the paws of the great sphinx of Khafre stands an impressive monument. It is higher than a man and is inscribed with the words of Thutmose IV. The inscription is an attempt to justify the king's rise to power.

According to this account, at that time the paws of the sphinx were covered with sand. King Thutmose IV had a dream in which he was told that if he would remove the sand, he would be given the throne. He removed the sand and was accepted as the rightful ruler.

It seems more likely that his older brother had been struck down during the tenth plague, leaving him to inherit the kingdom.

---

1. James Henry Breasted, *Ancient Records of Egypt*, Historical Documents (New York: Russell and Russell, 1906; reprinted 1962), 2:149:2.

2. This was the first obelisk to be erected in Rome after the establishment of Christianity, and set a precedent for Rome's borrowing of Christianity from Egypt.

3. For a discussion of the obelisks, see Labib Habachi, *The Obelisks of Egypt: Skyscrapers of the Past* (New York: Columbia U. Press, 1985).

4. This is the position adopted by the *Seventh-day Adventist Bible Commentary*, vol. 1, 191, 192.

5. *The International Standard Bible Encyclopedia*, s.v., "Exodus, Date of the." An expanded view of the Exodus by Shea is found in his *EXODUS*, an unpublished manuscript of 110 pages, including a ten-page bibliography with references.

6. J. E. Harris, and K. R. Weeks, *X-Raying the Pharaohs* (New York: Scribners, 1973), 138.

7. See also D. B. Redford, "The Coregency of Thutmose III and Amenhophis II," *Journal of Egyptian Archaeology*, 51:108-122.

Chapter 10

The Date of the Exodus

Although biblical scholars were originally in almost total agreement with a Bible chronology that placed the Exodus at about 1450 B.C., over time, opinion shifted, and the Exodus was assigned to a period during the reign of Rameses II, two hundred years later. Rameses II was said to be the pharaoh of the oppression and his son Merneptah the pharaoh of the Exodus. Today most scholars and commentaries accept the later date for the Exodus.

Mounting evidence, however, favors the earlier date. Inside the Cairo Museum there stands an eight-foot-high monument commemorating Pharaoh Merneptah (1227-1217 B.C.). It is known as the "Merneptah Stele." On it the name of Israel appears. A part of the inscription reads, "Israel is laid waste, his seed is not."

This is the first mention of Israel on an ancient monument. The date of the Stele is 1220 B.C., offering proof that Israel was already in Palestine before that time. This being so, Rameses II (c. 1295-1223 B.C.) could not have been the pharaoh of the oppression and his son Merneptah the pharaoh of the Exodus. Also, Merneptah reigned only a few years, so he could not have encountered the Israelites in Palestine if he were the pharaoh of the Exodus, because Israel wandered around in the wilderness and did not enter Palestine until forty years after the Exodus.

Some scholars have considered the Merneptah account little more than an illusion with little basis in fact, and so have not taken this reference seriously. However, during the winter of 1976-77, a war panel of Merneptah was discovered carved into the outside wall of the Karnak temple just to the right of the peace treaty entered into between Rameses II and the Hittites. Here, according to the interpretation of Frank J. Yurco, who studied the site, the identical Canaanite campaign referred to in the Merneptah Stele is described.

According to Yurco, not only does the name Israel appear just as it does on the Merneptah Stele, but the Israelites are visually portrayed. This depiction of the Israelites of the thirteenth century B.C., if the interpretation by Yurco is correct, is six hundred years earlier than their next appearance. Then, they were depicted on the wall of the Assyrian king Sennacherib's (704-681 B.C.) palace in reliefs of the siege and battle of the Israelite city of Lachish.[1]

The pharaoh who changed gods

Also throwing light on the date of the Exodus is the unusual reign of Amenhotep IV, better known as Akhenaten, the heretic king. His wife was the equally famous Nefertiti. His heresy stemmed from his rejection of the traditional worship of Amon and the gallery of Egyptian gods. He replaced the worship of many gods with the worship of just one god—Aton, the sun disc. Hence his name was changed from Amenhotep—honoring the god Amon, to Akhenaten—honoring Aton the sun god.

On my first visit to Karnak, I was shown a large field of inscribed bricks. These bricks had once formed a great temple dedicated to the sun that was erected at Karnak by Akhenaten. When I returned after a few years, the bricks had disappeared, but several years later I discovered them in the great Amon Temple of Luxor, a couple of miles to the south.

I accidentally came across them stored in a special enclosure, out of bounds to tourists, adjacent to the outside wall of the temple. There they were, row upon row, thousands of inscribed bricks that had once formed the majestic sun temple of Akhenaten.

And herein lies the story of the greatest computer feat ever attempted, at least to that time—the visual reconstruction of this famous temple of Akhenaten. The bricks that had been moved from Karnak to Luxor were all photographed and recorded in a computer. The photographs were then assembled on the computer screen to form a picture of the once spectacular sun temple of Akhenaten.[2]

According to the computerized reconstruction, the Akhenaten temple that had stood at Karnak was adorned with a likeness of the striking rays of the sun reaching out in blessing to the king and his royal family.

But the magnificent temple of Akhenaten and traditional capital at Karnak were abandoned for a new site at Tell el-Amarna 260 miles to the north. Here Akhenaten, the Sun King, laid out an entirely new capital city. He called it Akhetaten—"the horizon of the [sun disk] Aton." The entire city of Akhetaten was dedicated to the sun. Here Akhenaten lived with his beautiful wife Nefertiti and his six daughters.

Lavish living in Sun City

Leaving Cairo, the local pastor and I drove the 190 miles to the site of the sand-buried city of Akhenaten, a royal capital built and abandoned in a single generation. We crossed the Nile by boat to the western side, where we boarded a covered wagon pulled by a tractor. We were taken a short distance across the desert sand to the excavated remains of a temple dedicated to Nefertiti.

A further ride, seated on the tractor, took us for several miles across the dust dunes that covered the ancient metropolis of Akhetaten, a city that once extended for eight miles along the western banks of the Nile. Although blowing sands had long since obscured most of the work of the archaeologists, there were ample indications of their presence.

The famous Sun City of Akhenaten is now identified as Tell el-Amarna. The city had consisted of well-laid-out streets and boulevards, and magnificent palaces and temples. Beyond the southern outskirts of the main town, the king had laid out his pleasure park with two large, walled-in gardens, one of which included a shallow boating lake 125 yards long. Here Akhenaten, the Sun King, lived in comfort, luxury, and ease, while his empire crumbled away.

Soon after Akhenaten's death, the buildings were torn down and the mud bricks carried off for use elsewhere. The walls were often plastered with manure to dry in the sun for use as fuel, a custom still followed in primitive villages. Through the centuries the local peasants dug away the ancient walls to manure their fields.

All traces of the city had vanished for millennia when, in 1887, a peasant woman was digging away at the refuse and rubbish of an old settlement. Her little tools unexpectedly unearthed some old clay tablets with strange markings on them. Thinking they might have some value, she chucked them into several old gunny sacks and sold them to a neighboring villager for a few pennies. He threw the sacks over the back of his donkey and bumped his way along the bank of the Nile for 190 miles to Cairo. But the antique dealers, believing the tablets to be forgeries, weren't interested. So he hauled them back, breaking many of them in transport.

Still persistent, he then took the sacks of tablets all the way to Luxor, another 160 miles. Here at last an antique dealer recognized their true value and purchased them.

The strange tablets were soon bought by the museums in Berlin and London and studied by the scholars. And what a message they bore! They included a whole library of diplomatic correspondence between the Egyptian king Akhenaten and the kings of city-states in Palestine and Syria. These letters reveal that Canaan was in a state of chaos. Egyptian power in the area was falling apart. Among other things, the "Habiru" were overrunning the country of Palestine. And the kings of the Palestine city-states were wondering why Akhenaten would do nothing about it.

The "Habiru" are, of course, the Hebrews. In the Old Testament, the term *Hebrew* is usually used by foreigners speaking of Israel, or by Israel when they spoke of themselves to foreigners. The king of Jerusalem wrote:

> Let the king turn his attention to the archers, and let the king, my lord, send out troops of archers, (for) the king has no lands (left)! The 'Apiru [Habiru] plunder all the lands of the king. If there are archers (here) in this year, the lands of the king, my lord, will remain (intact); but if there are no archers (here), the lands of the king, my lord, will be lost!"[3]

There is no evidence that the lord, King Akhenaten, lounging in his palace, ever responded.

The tablets are of immense value. Here we have firsthand evidence of conditions in Canaan in the fourteenth century B.C. We also have evidence of the earlier date for the Exodus. For if the Exodus had not occurred until the later period of Rameses the Great, the "Habiru" would not have been in Canaan for at least another century.

The treasures of King Tutankhamen

One of Akhenaten's daughters was married to youthful Tutankhamen, who was probably then under ten years of age. He soon succeeded Akhenaten to the throne. The discoveries from King Tut's now famous tomb help immensely to illuminate this period.

King Tutankhamen was buried in the Valley of the Kings on the western side of the Nile, where Egyptian kings were buried over a period of some six hundred years.

The amazing story of the discovery of Tut's tomb begins in 1817 with the finding of the tomb of Seti I. Seti I succeeded Rameses I to the throne in 1317 B.C. Seti's conquests into

Palestine are depicted on the outside wall of the great Hypostyle Hall at Karnak.

Seti's tomb is a major tourist attraction. The corridors and chambers are decorated with artistic reliefs associated with the afterlife. They lead more than three hundred feet underground to the Golden Hall, where the king's huge sarcophagus was found.

At the time of the discovery, his mummy and all the treasures were missing. Sixty-four years later, however, his mummy and a cluster of thirty-five more were found in a deep pit on the slopes of the hills of Dahr el-Bahri, near the mortuary temple of Hatshepsut.

Seventeen years after that, the tomb of Amenhotep II was opened; it contained his mummy and twelve others. Today they form a novel display in the mummy room of the Cairo Museum.

Through the years, additional tombs were found. Between the years 1903 and 1909 the American archaeologist Theodore Davis, assisted at times by Howard Carter, unearthed sixteen tombs. But after that, all was a blank. He ends his preface describing his last excavation with the words, "I fear that the Valley of the Kings is now exhausted."

But Carter thought otherwise. Some funerary articles had been found bearing the name of King Tutankhamen, good evidence that his tomb must be in the area. Securing the financial help of Lord Canarvon, Carter was eager to continue the dig when the Davis concession reverted to him in 1914. Delayed by the war, it was not until 1917 that the real campaign for the illusive tomb began. But six fruitless years passed by. Two hundred thousand tons of sand and rubbish were removed, but without success.

After considerable reluctance, Canarvon agreed to one last winter's work. "One!" he repeated. That would finish it. The only area so far untouched by their work was at the foot of the tomb of Rameses VI where stood the remains of the old tool room used by the builders of his tomb, within a yard of the very spot where the work had begun.

"Tear it down," was Carter's order, "and dig there."

Directly beneath were steps. They led down to a tomb door and, beyond the door, into a corridor and a second door.

Peeping through a small hole into the chamber beyond, Carter was literally transfixed and speechless at what he saw. Lord Canarvon, growing impatient, cried out, "Do you see anything? Do you see anything?"

"Yes," was the response, "wonderful things!"

The tomb was filled with more than 2,200 objects, valued at over twelve million dollars. This is all the more remarkable when we consider that Tutankhamen was a young, insignificant king who reigned only eight years and died at about age eighteen. Think of the treasures the larger tombs must once have contained!

The discovery of Tut's tomb full of treasure helps us to understand and appreciate more fully the words about Moses in the book of Hebrews:

> By faith Moses, when he was come to years, refused to be called the son of Pharaoh's daughter; choosing rather to suffer affliction with the people of God, than to enjoy the pleasures of sin for a season; esteeming the reproach of Christ greater riches than the treasures in Egypt: for he had respect unto the recompense of the reward. By faith he forsook Egypt, not fearing the wrath of the king: for he endured, as seeing him who is invisible (Hebrews 11:24-27).

Moses could have fallen heir to immeasurable wealth. He could be a royal mummy under one of the glass cases in the mummy room of the Cairo Museum, but he passed it by for the better choice.

Where is Moses now? Resurrected from the grave as a representative of all who shall at Christ's return come forth from the dust, he stands with Jesus in the heavenly courts.

When on the Mount of Transfiguration Jesus stood with Peter, James, and John, it was Moses, along with Elijah, who came to encourage Him as He faced the cross (see Luke 9:30, 31).

---

1. Frank J. Yurco, "3,200-Year-Old Picture of Israelites Found in Egypt," *BAR*, September/October 1990, 20-37; see also F. Yurko, "Merneptah's Palestinian Campaign," *SSEA Journal (Society for the Study of Egyptian Antiquities)*, May 1978, 1.

2. *National Geographic*, November 1970, 634-655.

3. Pritchard, *The Ancient Near East*, 270.

Chapter 11

From Egypt to Sinai

A caravan of eleven taxis pulled away from the Alexander Young Hotel in Cairo. We were on a study tour of the Bible lands with Dr. Siegfried H. Horn of Andrews University.

After only six miles of travel, we were in the desert, a strong hint of what lay before us. The taxis were in fairly decent condition. Experienced Egyptian drivers would guide us on our journey to Mt. Sinai, following the same tortuous wilderness route over which Israel walked so long ago.

Eighty miles of dreary desert brought us to the city of Suez and the Suez Canal. While passports were checked and further travel arrangements negotiated, we spent several hours checking out the town and enjoying lunch in an air-conditioned hotel. We then traveled a few miles north to the ferry dock, where we would be crossing the famed canal.

We then crossed over on a tiny ferry, three cars at a time—a crossing that took us from the continent of Africa to the continent of Asia. On the opposite shore, we turned south and followed the course of the canal toward the Gulf of Suez and the Red Sea. It was already past two o'clock in the afternoon, and the unfriendly sun beat down on us.

Our first stop was at Ayun Musa—the Well of Moses—a pool about seventy-five feet across. It is surrounded by palm trees, which offered a bit of welcome shade while the taxis, with their hoods raised, cooled off.

Our journey took us along a narrow strip of pavement, rather straight and flat at first, but then more mountainous. The road twisted among jagged ridges and sandy mounds. Occasional side roads led to rich oil fields.

Increasing winds hit us like a blast furnace as we traveled through the Wilderness of Shur toward Marah, our next stop. *Marah* means "bitter." Here the bitter water was made sweet for Israel's already weary multitudes (see Exodus 15:23-25). Here we again waited twenty minutes or so for the motors to cool. So it would be for the rest of the journey—about twenty minutes of driving, followed by twenty minutes for cooling off the motors.

A few more miles, past more rugged mountains and ravines, brought us to Elim. Here Israel found twelve wells of water and seventy palm trees (see Exodus 15:27). For us it was the first place with drinkable water since leaving Suez, and the palms still offered welcome shade. Our thoughts were on the Israelites and the trials they encountered.

At about five o'clock, we emerged from the mountains, carved with canyons and crevices, into a large plain bordering on the blue waters of the sea. Nineteen white tents had been prepared for us, and here we spent the night, lulled to sleep by the waters washing on the shore.

That evening, Dr. Horn read to us from Numbers 33:10 and 11. Describing Israel's journey, it reports:

> And they removed from Elim, and encamped by the Red Sea. And they removed from the Red Sea, and encamped in the Wilderness of Sin.

This is the only site between Elim and the Wilderness of Sin with an open space by the sea. We were no doubt camping on the very spot where Israel made their encampment.

The mines of Sinai

In the area to the east of here, somewhat north of Mount

Sinai, Flinders Petrie, in 1905 and 1906, discovered some ancient copper and turquoise mines. For a number of miles we had been following the ancient route leading to these mines. Of special significance was the discovery by Petrie of inscribed pieces of stone now known as the Sinaitic Inscription.

Before this discovery, scholars had contended that Moses could not have written the first five books of the Bible, because at that early date there was no alphabetic script. And without it, the task of writing these lengthy books would have been virtually impossible. The Sinaitic Inscription on stone changed the minds of even the most liberal scholars. For its language proved to be an alphabetic script dating back to at least 1600 B.C.—long before Moses would have needed it. The writing was apparently that of the Canaanites employed to work in the Egyptian mines of the area.

Other ancient alphabetic scripts have since been found, and today all scholars agree that Moses did, indeed, have access to an alphabetic script.

The walls of these mines at Sinai were often inscribed with Egyptian inscriptions. In 1960, however, near some Egyptian inscriptions, another Canaanite inscription was discovered using the same alphabetic script as the Sinaitic Inscription. As translated by Dr. William Shea, it reads: "Now for the congregation and Hobab, mighty is the furnace."[1]

The inscription was obviously a memorial to a furnace. Significantly, nearby lay an immense pile of slag, the result of copper smelting. Petrie described a pile of slag eight feet high running along a valley about three hundred feet wide and five hundred feet long. He quotes a German geologist who saw it before his day: "Besides this mass of slag, which may amount to about 100,000 tons, I saw much scattered slag all the way up the tablet."[2]

This slag was from a smelting furnace, no doubt the furnace referred to in the text. But what need was there for such a large amount of bronze?

The Old Testament speaks of bronze 130 times, thirty-five times in the last chapters of Exodus in reference to the construction of the tabernacle. It is estimated that up to two and one-half tons of bronze were used in the tabernacle and its furnishings.

Could this furnace be the one used by the Israelites when God directed them to build the tabernacle?

The inscription mentions the "congregation." Although the word *Israel* does not appear, this term is used frequently to refer to the congregation of Israel.

There is further evidence. Reference is made to Hobab. He was the son of Jethro and was Moses' brother-in-law (see Numbers 10:29). Moses asked him to serve as the guide for their journey. Furthermore, Hobab was a Kennite, and the principal activity of the Kennites was the smelting of copper.

So, amazing as it may seem, it is very probable that this inscription is a memorial set up by the Israelites to commemorate the furnace used to smelt the bronze for their tabernacle.

Immediately following the June 1967 Six-Day War that gave Sinai to the Jews, Sinai became an archaeological treasure trove. During the next fifteen years, from 1967 to 1982, dozens of expeditions were launched and hundreds of ancient mining sites located, some of them dating to the third millennium B.C. Apparently the Sinai Peninsula had teemed with mining activity.[3] Mined by the Egyptians from the twentieth to the twelfth centuries B.C., a period of eight hundred years, these sites were the only source of turquoise in the eastern Mediterranean.

Into the wilderness

Back on our route, we soon entered the Wilderness of Sin, a barren plain twenty-five miles across and seemingly without a blade of vegetation. Our sympathies went out to the complaining Israelites.

It was here that God first miraculously provided them with manna, a certain amount each day, just enough for the day, except that on the sixth day they received a double portion—enough to carry them over the Sabbath, when none fell (see Exodus 16:21-30).

Fortunately, having broken camp at 5:00 a.m., our drive through the wearisome plain was in the freshness of the early morning. The return trip would be in mid-afternoon, with the dust blowing and the sun scorching like a blast oven.

As the sun peeped over the mountaintops, we emerged from the Wilderness of Sin and turned eastward toward the interior. Here we left the oil-surfaced road we had been following and entered the Wadi Feiran—a dry riverbed most of the year, but a raging torrent in time of rain. It followed a valley, usually about half a mile wide. Ravines and lesser wadis broke out in different directions, but only one would take us to Mount Sinai.

By following this route, it is possible to point to several stations along the route that correspond to those mentioned in the Bible. That this is impossible for any other route is good evidence that we were following the true path of the Israelites.

Along the way, the drivers would choose their ruts, gun their cars in second gear, and drive like fury to avoid getting stuck. They were also generally fighting for the lead as though running the Indianapolis 500 race.

En route, we could see the heights of Mount Serbal to our left, the site of some of the mining operations. Shortly after nine o'clock, we arrived at the traditional site of Rephidim, where the children of Israel were attacked by the Amalekites (see Exodus 17:8-13). A few of us clambered to the top of a mountain peak overlooking the valley to stand where Moses stood while the battle raged.

Rephidim was the only oasis we passed after leaving Elim, and Elim was hardly worthy of the name. Today, Rephidim houses a small Bedouin community. After considerable urging, we finally gained permission to photograph a Bedouin woman in her colorful attire, her head and face completely covered.

A few miles down the road, we came upon a caravan of camels returning from a mission on which they had picked up a bride for one of the men back home. It must have been just the same when Eleizer brought Rebekah to Isaac. Customs haven't changed much in these remote areas.

Only occasional scrub tamarisk shrubs marked our way as the journey continued. Then a grove of them appeared. While waiting for the motors to cool, we sang together, "It's Not Far to Canaan's Land."

At times, cars would get stuck in the soft sand, and we would give the necessary push. Often the cars would stop until all had caught up, just to make sure none were missing. At one point, one of the cars had to be abandoned. Extra room, however, had been provided in the other vehicles for such an emergency.

Often it appeared as though the way would be blocked; then a pass would open up before us. Coming through one such pass, we entered a great plain—the first since the Wilderness of Sin. From pictures we had seen, we recognized a little white chapel atop a mound—we had come to the Golden Calf Knoll, sight of Israel's great apostasy. A short distance beyond, we looked up at Sinai, the once sacred mount. We had traveled uphill all the way, so at the base of Mount Sinai we had climbed to five thousand feet.

Saint Catherine's monastery

A road through a narrow ravine took us to the left of the towering heights of Mount Sinai, past a well-watered garden, to the famed Saint Catherine's monastery. There we stood amazed before its massive protective walls, five feet thick, dating back to Justinian of the sixth century. The emperor had it erected on the site where Helena, the mother of Constantine, had built a small church two centuries before.

Founded in the fourth century, Saint Catherine's is one of the oldest monasteries in the world that is still in use. During past centuries the wall had no gateway. The only entrance was a small opening high on the wall. A basket and hoist transported visitors to the entrance.

The stout walls enclose a great complex of buildings, one of them with a tall, white minaret. The clever monks erected a mosque within the complex in the seventh century, thus assuring protection during the Arab raids against the Christians. Their efforts proved successful, for it was the only monastery to survive.

We were met very cordially by the Greek Orthodox priest, who escorted us to the second floor of a modest dormitory— our sleeping quarters for the next two nights.

We had not eaten since 4:30 that morning. It was now two in the afternoon, so we gathered in the dining hall for our lunch, all of which was catered from Cairo and brought with us, as was our Arab cook.

A period of rest and leisure was followed by a tour through the monastery buildings. Saint Catherine was a Christian hermit who lived near Alexandria in Egypt. The monks believe that her body was transported by angels to this spot.

Passing through the Chapel of Saint Catherine, we stood in awe beneath the glitter of the Church of the Transfiguration. In the apse, we looked up at the magnificently painted dome from the sixth century. In the court, we saw the well where the water was drawn for the monks. Then, walking through the corridors, we passed the bakery.

We were especially interested in the monastery library, one of the most famous in the world. There we viewed hundreds of priceless icons. The icon of Saint Peter is said to be one of the most beautiful ever produced.

What has contributed most to the library's fame, however, are its three thousand ancient manuscripts. An old monk with flowing white hair and beard showed us the famous Codex Sinaitic Syriac of the fourth or fifth century, neatly packed inside a wooden chest in a glass case. Also inside the chest were several famous letters—including one from Mohammed and another from Napoleon.

Of still greater importance, it was here in 1844 that Constantin Tischendorf discovered the most famous Bible manuscript—the Codex Sinaiticus, now in the British Museum.

Tischendorf found the monks throwing leaves of the manuscript into the fireplace and was able to rescue them for posterity. The priceless pages date back to the fourth century.

In the library, it is possible to read sermons written in the fourth century. Recent years have seen new manuscripts of major significance come to light. Also, the precious library manuscripts have been put on microfilm.

Continuing our tour, we were directed to the purported burning bush, a rather insignificant little bush a few feet high, growing near a wall. It is believed by the monks to be the very one from which God spoke to Moses. For every incident recorded in the Bible, a traditional site seems to have been established, and pious but gullible pilgrims believe them to be genuine.

Entering the monastery gardens, we were led to a small white building—the charnel, or bone house. Beside it stands the local cemetery. It is only a few feet in dimension, so the body of the deceased remains buried in this plot for only six years, after which it is removed and the bones placed inside the building.

Inside the doorway, posted as a guard, sits Saint Stephen of about A.D. 1300. His skeleton is draped with his monkish robes. The room is piled high with the bones of the priests who lived out their lives in this sacred spot. Once they come here, it is for life.

Climbing Mount Sinai

The highlight of our visit was the hike up Sinai, the once holy mount. It was early to bed and early to rise, for we picked up the trail at the monastery at six o'clock the following morning. Twenty minutes up the steep path through a ravine took us to Saint Stephen's Chapel, where, we were told, Saint

Stephen sat to receive confessions and to receive tolls from pious pilgrims. A few minutes more, and we passed through Saint Stephen's Gate, "the Gate of Heaven."

All the way, the trail was laid out with neatly placed stone steps, the work of the monks who have inhabited the area through the years, one of them giving seventy years of his life to the project. Three thousand feet of steady climbing amid the massive limestone cliffs took us to the Meadow of Elijah. A small white chapel stands over what is said to be the cave in which the prophet found shelter when fleeing from Jezebel. Another chapel covers the traditional hollow of the rock that sheltered Moses as the glory of the Lord passed before him.

Up to this point it is possible for the less hearty to come by camel along a special trail. The camels were taking this particular day off, however, it being a Muslim holy day.

Another thousand feet up, the peak of Jebul Musa towered before us. By nine-thirty the last of our group had arrived, and Pastor Neal Wilson, who had joined our group in Cairo, led out in a memorable service of consecration beside the little stone chapel that crowns the summit.

There were forty-five in our group, plus several others from Beirut and Egypt who joined us—most of them ministers of the gospel, many of them college or university professors. They had come from the United States, Canada, South America, Europe, and South Africa. The international nature of the group was highlighted by prayer responses from nine persons from as many different countries, each praying in his native tongue.

Jebul Musa, meaning "Mountain of Moses," 7,500 feet in elevation, is the chief peak of this Sinai Peninsula mountain range. From its summit, however, the landscape below in every direction is one of rugged ridges and ravines, affording no view of the open plain where Israel was camped.

The impressive peak at the beginning of the mountain range, rising directly from the valley and usually identified as Mount Sinai in pictures, is of Ras es-SafSaf. With an elevation of 6,830 feet, it rises 1,870 feet above the plain. No steps, however, or path of any kind, lead to its summit. Nevertheless, nineteen of us chose to make the additional climb.

Our climb took us back to the Meadow of Elijah, then off in another direction, up steep inclines, over great boulders and through narrow passes. We were ever hoping that we were going in the right direction. At one point the hardiest of our group mounted a summit, only to call back to the rest of us that the mount we sought was still beyond.

At last we reached the summit—a sight to remember. Far below, on the great plain before us, Israel must have made their camp. Although the exact site cannot be determined, somewhere on this mountain Moses must have stood. Here he met with God. Amid thunder, lightning, and earthquake, God spoke His Holy Law of Ten Commandments, then delivered them to Moses on two tablets of stone. Here, also, Moses received instructions for building the tabernacle and for conducting its services—a miniature of the gospel that points to the cross of Christ and His ministry in the heavenly sanctuary.

As I viewed the plain, I thought of what Dr. Horn had read to us in our devotion the evening before, speaking of Israel's entrance onto this plain:

> Through one of the deep, gravelly passes they were now led. . . . And now before them in solemn majesty Mount Sinai lifted its massive front.[4]

I was faced with the opportunity of a lifetime. I determined to cross the plain and see if such a description could be verified. After descending from Sinai, I returned to Saint Catherine's, grabbed a sandwich, and began to cross the plain. Focusing my eyes ahead, the mountains surrounding the valley seemed to converge. But at the far end, they overlapped. I walked through the deep, gravelly pass that was the only approach from the far side of the plain. I turned around and began walking toward the mount. And "now before [me] in solemn majesty Mount Sinai lifted its massive front."

The description given by the author of this quotation is correct. The author must have been inspired.

1. William H. Shea, "Dedicated to a Furnace," *Ministry*, 5 September 1989. For a fuller description of the linguistic and archaeological details involved in this study, see the author's "New Light on the Exodus and on Construction of the Tabernacle: Gerster's Proto-Sinaitic Inscription No. 1," *Andrews University Seminary Studies*, 25 (Spring 1987): 73-96.
2. Shea, 6.
3. Itzhaq Beit-Arieh, "Fifteen Years in Sinai—Israeli Archaeologists Discover a New World," *BAR*, July/August 1984, 25-54.
4. Ellen G. White, *Patriarchs and Prophets* (Hagerstown, Md.: Review and Herald Publishing Association, 1958), 301.

Chapter 12

Israel's Footsteps in the Wilderness

After almost a year at the foot of Mount Sinai, the children of Israel were summoned for their march to Canaan, the Promised Land. The route they followed led them first to its southern borders, a distance they could have made in about eleven days. Because of unbelief, however, they were not permitted to enter Canaan, but were forced to wander about for another forty years in the northern area of the Sinai Peninsula known as the Negev.

One summer, I was one of a group that spent two days in this lonely desert with Dr. Nelson Glueck, noted for the many years he spent exploring the valley of the Jordan and this vast wilderness area. His fascinating work is reported in his popular books, *The River Jordan* and *Rivers in the Desert: A History of the Negev*.[1]

Our first day took us twenty-five miles south of Beer-sheba to Shivta (Isbeita), the site of an imposing mound, crowned with ancient ruins. It was difficult to imagine that these ruins were once a thriving community of up to five thousand inhabitants.

We walked over to a large cistern with water visible below, and Glueck explained how survival was possible in that remote desert area. Each settlement had its well, or cistern, usually roofed over. Glueck had located hundreds of them. They were coated with layers of plaster, firmed with bits of pottery. Frequently, natural caves would be enlarged and used as cisterns. In these cisterns, water would keep from one year to the next.

But where did the water come from? Dr. Glueck had the answer. The surrounding hills were lined with courses of rocks that had been laid in such a way as to form channels that would guide the water to the settlements. As we traveled, Dr. Glueck pointed them out to us. Sometimes the water would be brought in from as far as ten miles away. Rainfall was scanty, but through this unique system every drop was utilized to the best advantage.

We made our way up a path to the top of the mound. We walked along ancient streets, about twelve feet wide, with the remains of dwellings on either side—some of them two stories high. There were three churches with their apses and columns still standing. Two baptisteries gave evidence of their having been used for baptism by immersion.

The ruins we saw were of Byzantine origin from the fifth and sixth centuries A.D., but they covered more ancient remains. Glueck suggested four periods of population: (1) the time of Abraham, from the twenty-first to nineteenth centuries B.C.; (2) the Judean period from the tenth to the sixth centuries B.C.; (3) the period of the Nabataeans from the sixth century B.C. to A.D. 106; (4) the Byzantine period in the fifth and sixth centuries A.D.

The second day we traveled to Abdah (Eboda). Its remains are impressive. A massive mound is crowned by the walls of a great Byzantine castle and monastery. On the slopes we saw huge vats, a striking evidence of the productivity of the surrounding vineyards. We were especially interested in the brick kiln, or oven, of Nabataean origin. Here the Nabataeans baked their unique pottery. Nabataean potsherds lay on the ground. Beneath the ruins of the monastery, Glueck had uncovered the foundations of a large Nabataean temple.

Abdah, forty miles south of Beer-sheba, was once a principal trading center on the main route between Arabia and the Mediterranean. The Nabataean fortress was captured by the Romans in A.D. 106, bringing the Nabataean kingdom to an end.

Before returning to Beer-sheba, we drove another fourteen miles southwest of Abdah to view the impressive Mitzpa Ramon. This great and colorful miniature of the Grand Canyon of the Colorado is twenty miles long and five miles wide. An international sculptural society had recently held their world congress here and had left sculpted monuments to mark their presence.

Recalling Israel's journey, Moses said, "When we departed from Horeb, we went through all that great and terrible wilderness . . . and we came to Kadesh Barnea" (Deuteronomy 1:19).

Kadesh-Barnea served as the principal site of Israel's encampment during their wanderings. The probable site, several miles east, was excavated between 1976 and 1979.[2]

Rose-red Petra

After the congregation had wandered in the wilderness for forty years, God led Israel along a well-traveled route to the Promised Land. They traveled over the ancient King's Highway, which was the main route north. This took them north past Edom and then through the Arnon and Zered Canyons to Transjordan, the area east of the Jordan River.

On their journey, Israel sought permission to pass through the land of the Edomites but were refused. At that time the capital city of the Edomites was Selah. Centuries later, at the base of Selah, the Nabataeans in the third century B.C. constructed their capital city of Petra, one of earth's most colorful and unusual cities. Carved out of deep pink rock, Petra has been characterized, since Dean Burgon of Newgate coined the phrase in 1845, "the rose-red city half as old as time."

Petra is surrounded by colorful sandstone mountains. We entered Petra by horseback through a narrow, mile-long passage cut in the colorful rock. Varying from about seven to twenty feet wide, and extending upward from two hundred to three hundred feet, it forms the only entrance into this mysterious, hidden city.

The red-rock mountains of Petra are carved with hundreds of temples, tombs, and dwellings. Our provisions, catered in by the Philadelphia Hotel of Amman, included two large, white tents—one to serve as the kitchen and the other as the dining room. Our sleeping quarters for the two nights we were there were in the ancient rock-cut chambers. Since modern hotels now serve the tourists, several of the chambers have been converted into souvenir shops.

This city cut out of rock was originally a stronghold of the Horites, who were driven out by the Edomites. The Edomites were the descendants of Esau, the brother of Jacob. The Edomites were in turn dispossessed by the Nabataeans, who developed Petra into a principal trading center along the main caravan route from Mesopotamia and Syria to Arabia and Egypt. Petra declined only after the Romans diverted the trade route from Petra to Palmyra in Syria.

Through the centuries, Petra was considered a sacred place and out of bounds to infidels. In 1812 the Swiss explorer, John Burckhardt, was the first in modern times to enter the strange and mysterious city. He did so by disguising himself as an Arab in search of the tomb of Aaron.

After Burckhardt, only a few daring explorers ventured in. Even then, for years those entering could do so only with armed guards, and some never returned. Not until after World War I was Petra accessible to any except the most intrepid.

The highlight of our visit was a hike up to the top of the Mount of the High Place, where one of the most fascinating ruins of the Middle East is found. The ancient open-air sanctuary is approached by way of two obelisk-shaped sun pillars, thirty feet tall, cut from solid rock. Such pillars were worshiped by the pagan nations, and the Israelites were commanded to destroy them.

The high place consists of an open court twenty by sixty feet. In the center is a raised platform on which human and animal sacrifices were slain. A stone bench provided a place to prepare the animals burned on the altar. Several steps lead to the altar where the sacrifices were offered.

Climbing Selah—citadel of the Edomites

Petra is the capital of Edom. In the Old Testament, it is called Selah, which means "rock." The citadel stood on the platformlike top of a very conspicuous mountain at the far end of the valley. From the valley floor, this mountain looks like a gigantic rock. The top is reached only by a single, hardly discernible trail and is so rugged that few attempt the climb.

Only the most agile of our group accepted the challenge— the first group, we were told, to make the ascent in six years. We found pottery on the mountain's lofty heights that gave evidence of the Edomite presence. We also peered into large cisterns that had provided them with water.

When an Arab with his traditional headdress asked me if I was ready to go down, I responded, "Yes, I would like to get back and take some more pictures."

"Follow me," he advised.

Assuming that he was a native guide, I responded. But after a hundred feet or so, I became suspicious. We were scaling down the side of the cliff in a most frightening fashion. It was certainly not the way we had ascended.

"Are you sure we are going the right way?" I asked.

"Follow me," was his only reply.

Shortly, we came to an impossible situation—a straight drop of more than a thousand feet.

In horror, I inquired, "How many times have you been up here?"

"Oh," he replied, "this is my first time."

Fortunately, God's angels were on duty. Otherwise, we could never have made it back to the top, where we joined the rest of the party for a safe return.

Our climb to the top of this rocklike mountain gave us a new appreciation of the words of the ancient prophets. Speaking of the Edomites and their lofty perch, Obadiah declared:

> Thou that dwellest in the clefts of the rock, whose habitation is high; . . . Though thou exalt thyself as the eagle, and though thou set thy nest among the stars, thence will I bring thee down (Obadiah 3, 4).

And Jeremiah warned:

> O thou that dwellest in the clefts of the rock, that holdest the height of the hill: though thou shouldest make thy nest as high as the eagle, I will bring thee down from thence, saith the Lord (Jeremiah 49:16).

Selah was the scene of one of the most dramatic battles of history. It occurred when Amaziah was king of Judah. Of it we read:

> Other ten thousand left alive did the children of Judah carry away captive, and brought them unto the top of the rock, and cast them down from the top of the rock, that they all were broken in pieces (2 Chronicles 25:12).

Our visit to Petra included a hike to the monastery temple of ed-Deir, 148 feet high. Higher than a fourteen-story building, it is carved out of solid rock.

Along the King's Highway

Israel's journey took them south by way of the port city of Ezion Geber to the famed "King's Highway." After turning north and being refused passage through Edom, they were forced to take a route up the Arabah, that great fault in which the Dead Sea lies. The Edomites were to be punished for their refusal to permit Israel to pass through any of their territory—a judgment witnessed to by the desolation of the area that is evident to this very day (see Jeremiah 49:7-22).

Reaching the southern tip of the Dead Sea, Israel turned eastward along the brook Zered, a narrow stream of water running through a deep gorge that formed the border between Edom and Moab.

Not wishing to join battle with Moab, Israel circled to the east of its territory. Moab's capital city was then at present-day Kerak, atop a mountain marked today by the remains of an immense Crusader castle, the largest ever constructed in the Near East.

During the time of Israel's kings, Moab's capital citadel was besieged by Israelite forces. The invasion led the king of Moab to believe the gods were angry with them. And to appease the angry gods, the Moabite king sacrificed his firstborn son on the wall of Kerak (see 2 Kings 3:27).

Traveling northward along the eastern border of Moab, Israel crossed over the river Arnon, which flows through an immense canyon, similar to the Grand Canyon in Arizona. Crossing the little stream at the bottom of the canyon brought Israel and their flocks and herds into the land of the Ammonites.

When Moab extended its border north, Dibon became its capital. In 1868, the famous Moabite Stone was found at Dibon, bearing the name of the Moabite king, Mesha. This was one of the first discoveries in Palestine to throw light on the Old Testament.

In 2 Kings 3:4 and 5 we read:

Mesha king of Moab was a sheepmaster, and rendered unto the king of Israel an hundred thousand lambs, and an hundred thousand rams, with the wool. But it came to pass, when Ahab was dead, that the king of Moab rebelled against the king of Israel.

The Moabite inscription reads in part: "Omri, king of Israel oppressed Moab and his son [Ahab] after him."

Not only does this stone prove that Mesha was not a fictitious character, but that Mesha paid tribute to Omri.

North of Dibon, at present-day Madeba, there stands a Greek Orthodox Church that has beneath its floor a beautiful mosaic of the oldest map of Jerusalem known today.

Crossing into Ammonite territory, Israel engaged in their first battle, defeating Sihon at his capital city of Heshbon. Andrews University sponsored an archaeological dig at the supposed site of Heshbon, beginning in 1968 and extending over a period of several years. Called the Madeba Plains Project, the dig has shifted recently to the nearby site of Tell el-Umeiri. In 1987, it produced a seal inscribed with the name of Thutmose III, the pharaoh who very likely drowned in the Red Sea at the time of the Exodus.

Continuing northward on the eastern side of the Jordan, Israel crossed the Jabok River. This brought them into the territory of Bashan. Here, Og, Bashan's giant king, came out against them. The battle resulted in Israel's second great victory, ending the first phase of Israel's conquest. They were now in possession of all of Transjordan, the area east of the Jordan between Bashan and the river Arnon.

In 1967, excavators were working on a mound slightly north of the Jabok River that is believed to be the ancient city of Penuel, where Jacob wrestled with the angel (see Genesis 32:22-24). They came across a plastered wall with an inscribed message written in three columns about 24 inches high and 15 1/2 inches wide. The meaning is still uncertain; however, scholars have agreed on the translation of the first line. The 2,600-year-old message begins, "Inscription/text/ book of/ Balaam son of Beor, the man who was a seer of the gods."[3]

Obviously, this is the Balaam of the book of Numbers—the apostate prophet of Israel who compromised with the Moabites and led Israel into corruption when they were on the borders of Canaan (see Numbers 22-24).

As Israel made preparations for the invasion of western

Palestine, Moses was told he would die and a successor was to take over. In humble obedience to God's direction, he climbed to the heights of Nebo. There God gave him a view of the land of Israel's inheritance. Then, in silent submission, he was laid to rest.

1. Nelson Glueck, *The River Jordan* (Westminster Press, 1946), 268 pp., and *Rivers in the Desert: A History of the Negev* (New York: Grove Press, 1959).

2. Rudolph Cohen, "Did I Excavate Kadesh-Barnea?" *BAR*, May/June 1981, 20-33.

3. André Lemaire, "Fragments From the Book of Balaam Found at Deir Alla," *BAR*, September/October 1985, 26-39.

Behistun Rock in Iran (p. 11).

**Flood tablet from the palace of
Ashurbanipal (p. 18).**

Monument of Nabonidus describing the rebuilding of the Ur tower (p. 39).

Residence of Haran village chief (p. 47).

Cemetery of Bab edh-Dhra, believed to be Gomorrah (p. 56).

Pyramids of Giza (p. 63).

Temple complex of Amon at Thebes (p. 73).

113

Excavated remains of Jericho (p. 128).

Canaanite altar at Megiddo (p. 134).

Pool of Gibeon (p. 142).

**Stepped stone ramparts that supported the Citadel of David
and later the palace of Solomon (p. 144).**

Solomon's gateway at Hazor (pp. 148, 149).

Sphinx gate at the Hittite capital of Boghazköy (pp. 165, 166).

Relief of King Shishak on Karnak temple wall (p. 154).

Mound of Nimrud with palace remains of Shalmaneser III in the foreground (p. 160).

Black Obelisk of Shalmaneser III with relief of Jehu, king of Israel (p. 161).

Entrance to restored palace of Ashurnasirpal at Nimrud (pp. 171, 172).

War machine of Tiglath-pileser III (pp. 173-175).

Sennacherib's seige of Lachish (pp. 183, 184).

Ashurbanipal's lion hunt (p. 191).

Lion on wall of Ishtar Processional Way in Babylon (p. 202).

Replica of entrance to Ishtar Gateway forming entrance to
the restored area of Babylon (pp. 211, 212).

Within restored Ishtar Gateway of Babylon (p. 212).

Restored walk along Procession Street in Babylon (p. 213).

Herod's amphitheater at Caesarea (p. 218).

Herod's aqueduct at Caesarea (p. 219).

Mazar excavations below the western temple wall (p. 226).

Entering Cave IV, site of the richest find of the
Dead Sea Scrolls (pp. 230, 231).

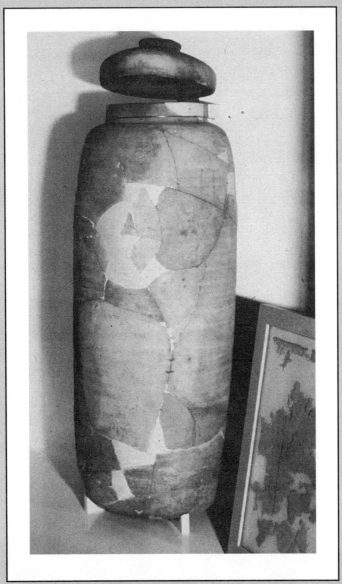

Pottery jar with scroll fragment (p. 230).

Mount Sinai (chapter 11).

Chapter 13

Crossing the Jordan

Following their conquest of Transjordan and the death of Moses, the Israelites made their way down into the great valley of the Jordan. Under their new leader, Joshua, they now faced the Jordan River, the most storied river on earth.

At the foot of Mount Hermon, four streams come together and flow down through the Jordan Valley into the Sea of Galilee, 685 feet below sea level. Flowing out of Galilee, the Jordan River continues south to the Dead Sea, a drop of another seven hundred feet. The Jordan River and the Dead Sea are in a great depression that begins in northern Syria and continues all the way south to the Red Sea.

Jordan means "arrow," and in the rainy season the river flows swiftly like an arrow, overflowing its banks. It is generally only about ninety to one hundred feet wide and three to ten feet deep. But it flows through a valley, the Ghor, meaning "depression," which is from four to thirteen miles wide. Within this depression is a lower depression called the Zor, meaning "thicket." The Bible speaks of it as "the jungle of the Jordan." And a jungle it was, filled with wild animals—elephants, hippos, rhinos, lions, bears, and other wildlife.

The Jordan Valley was called the "garden of God," the richest part of the country. The most populated area was that east of the Jordan. Little wonder that Reuben, Dan, and Manasseh chose it as their possession (see Numbers 32:1-6, 33).

The Jordan River winds through the valley like a serpent, with twists and turns of quarter, half, and three-quarter loops. When Israel crossed over, it was overflowing its banks, a raging torrent engulfing the depression.

The first city to fall before Israel was Jericho, the "city of palms."

Jericho has been thoroughly excavated. John Garstang, who dug there from 1930 to 1936, believed that he had found the walls of the ancient city, fallen flat just as indicated in the Bible. And he dated the destruction to about 1400 B.C.

Kathleen Kenyon, however, who excavated the site in the 1950s, disputed Garstang. She claimed as evidence to support her position that the Exodus had occurred under Rameses II in the thirteenth century B.C.

Through the years, conservative scholars who accepted the Bible chronology have believed Garstang was right. In a recent issue of *Biblical Archaeological Review*, Dr. Bryant Wood, a recognized ceramic expert, marshals a host of evidence from the recently published works authored by the late Kathleen Kenyon which, he believes, show that Garstang's earlier dating must have been right after all.[1] Kenyon, he observes, failed to give due consideration to much of her own evidence.

Her work, Wood points out, correlates with the biblical account in that: (1) the city was strongly fortified; (2) its destruction occurred after harvesttime in the spring; (3) the inhabitants had no opportunity to flee with their foodstuffs; (4) the siege was short; (5) the walls were leveled; (6) the city was plundered and burned.

To scholars, however, this poses a problem. As Wood puts it:

> One major problem remains: the date, 1400 B.C.E. Most scholars will reject the possibility that the Israelites destroyed Jericho in about 1400 B.C.E. because of their belief that Israel did not emerge in Canaan until about 150 to 200 years later, at the end of the late Bronze II period.

A minority of scholars agrees with the Biblical chronology, which places the Israelite entry into Canaan in about 1400 B.C.E. . . .

But recently, new evidence has come to light suggesting that Israel was resident in Canaan *throughout* the Late Bronze II period [1225-1200 B.C.]. As new data emerge and as old data are reevaluated, it will undoubtedly require a reappraisal of current theories regarding the *date* and the *nature* of the emergence of Israel in Canaan.[2]

Here, as Wood points out, the problem is that if the evidence of the Jericho excavations is accepted, suggesting the earlier date (1450 B.C.) for the Exodus, then the popular view assigning the Exodus to the period of Rameses II (c. 1295-1223 B.C.) cannot be correct and will have to be reevaluated. Such a reevaluation is long overdue.

In a subsequent issue of *Biblical Archaeological Review*, Wood's position is challenged by Piotr Bienkowski, curator of Egyptian and Near Eastern Antiquities at the National Museums and Galleries, Liverpool, England, to which Wood gives a very creditable rebuttal.[3] In the same issue, *BAR* editor Hershel Shanks gives a strong defense of Wood's scholarly credibility. Shanks also states, "Most scholars we have talked to do not disagree with Wood's dating of the evidence."[4] It is apparent that the trend today is back toward the mid-fifteenth century B.C. as the date for the Exodus, the date provided by the Bible itself (see 1 Kings 6:1).

The Promised Land

As you can tell by looking at a map of the land Israel entered, it is primarily hill country. Jerusalem, at about three thousand feet of elevation, lies on the top of the Judean ridge that parallels the Jordan Valley to the east. Crossing the Judean ridge west of Jerusalem, one enters the lowlands. Along the Mediterranean lies the Philistine Plain to the south and the Plain of Sharon to the north.

North of Jerusalem is the Carmel ridge with the Valley of Esdraelon at its feet. Beyond the Valley of Esdraelon to the north are the hills of Galilee.

The area is very small, barely larger than the state of Vermont. Though small, it had a geographical significance far out of proportion to its size, for it served as the land bridge connecting Mesopotamia and Egypt. All the ancient trade routes connecting Syria and Mesopotamia with Egypt and Arabia passed through her borders.

Along the west coast, the armies and traders followed the Way of the Sea.

The central route followed the Judean ridge. From the north, it passed southward through Shechem, Bethel, Jerusalem, and Hebron. This was the route Abraham followed when he came out of Ur.

The eastern route was along the King's Highway through Transjordan. It led through Bashan, Ammon, Moab, and Edom down to the port of Ezion Geber. This was the route Israel followed when they entered Canaan.

God placed Israel in this strategic location for a good reason. According to the promise made to Abraham and repeated to Isaac and Jacob, through the nation of Israel all the nations of earth were to be blessed. They were to uphold the worship of the true God and make Him known to all peoples. Here, at the crossroads of the world, they would have every advantage. Here they would come into contact with all nations.

Shortly after Israel's entrance into the land of Canaan and their initial conquests, they gathered at Shechem at God's command. There on the slopes of the mountains of Ebal and Gerizim, the covenant with Israel made at Sinai was renewed.

The Vale of Shechem is a nicely situated valley in the central hill country of Canaan. Here Abraham made his first stop upon entering Canaan, and here he built an altar.

Now, in harmony with God's instruction, Israel erected an altar of stone on Mount Ebal (see Deuteronomy 27:1-10). "Then Joshua built an altar unto the Lord God of Israel in mount Ebal" (Joshua 8:30).

Shechem discoveries

During excavations on Mount Ebal from 1982-84, an ancient altar was uncovered, believed to be the very one erected by Joshua. It is about fifteen by thirty feet and has a ramp twenty-three feet long and three feet wide.[5]

Shechem figured largely in the subsequent history of Israel. During the period of the Judges, Gideon's son, Abimelech, managed to set himself up as king in Shechem, but the people revolted. So Abimelech turned against them and burned the city, killing about a thousand who had found refuge in a tower.

Dr. G. Ernest Wright excavated at Shechem from 1956 to 1964. The excavations produced evidence that the city had been destroyed about 1125 B.C., the very period of Abimelech. It was yet another confirmation of the accuracy of Bible history.

While Dr. Siegfried Horn was associated with Dr. Wright in these excavations, they found the remains of a temple of that period, an enormous building, fifty-four by sixty-five feet, with walls six feet thick—no doubt the temple of Baal Berith. According to the Bible record, Abimelech used the money from this very temple to bribe vain persons to support him (see Judges 9:4).

Nearby, fronting the temple, was the stone pillar referred to in Joshua 9:4 and Judges 9:6 before which Israel had renewed their covenant with God. The excavations revealed that the temple had been destroyed by fire at the same time as the city.

The central and southern campaigns

After Israel offered a sacrifice of dedication at Shechem, the first area to be taken by the Israelites was the central hill country. And according to archaeological findings, it was the least populated at the time.

A few miles northwest of Jerusalem lies the Valley of Ajalon, where Joshua and the Gibeonites fought against the Amorites in the famous battle that Israel won because the sun stood still.

Israel took Lachish, whose king was assisted by the king of Gezer. They also took the land as far south as Hebron.

> So Joshua smote all the country of the hills, and of the south, and of the vale, and of the springs, and all their kings: he left none remaining, but utterly destroyed all that breathed, as the Lord God of Israel commanded. And Joshua smote them from Kadesh-barnea even unto Gaza, and all the country of Goshen, even unto Gibeon. And all these kings and their land did Joshua take at one time, because the Lord God of Israel fought for Israel (Joshua 10:40-42).

The northern campaign

A few miles north of the Sea of Galilee lay a little body of water known as the waters of Meron, now a fertile valley. Joshua, chapter 11, relates how the king of Hazor, hearing of what had happened to the south, gathered a coalition of northern kings at the "waters of Meron, to fight against Israel."

Verse 4 states that there were "much people, even as the sand that is upon the seashore in multitude, with horses and chariots very many." Despite their numbers, however, they were badly defeated by Israel. Then Joshua turned northward and destroyed Hazor.

Joshua 11:11 states that Joshua burned Hazor with fire. Excavations at Hazor give striking evidence of the fire. In a temple at Hazor excavators uncovered a charred beam that had fallen from the roof.

Of all the cities Joshua conquered, Hazor is the only one that was destroyed by fire, according to the Bible. And in the excavations, this is the only city that gives evidence of such destruction during this northern campaign.

Israel's tabernacle was set up at Shiloh, where it remained for three hundred years, finally suffering destruction by the Philistines in the battle of Aphek. During the battle the sacred ark was captured. That day Eli, the priest, and his two sons died (see 1 Samuel 4:11, 17, 18).

Although the actual site of the tabernacle at Shiloh has not been identified, excavations in the area have given ample evidence of the destruction at that time.[6]

As Joshua's life drew to a close, Israel gathered again at Shechem for another renewal of God's covenant with Israel. There Joshua rehearsed God's blessings to them:

> Not one thing hath failed of all the good things which the Lord God spake concerning you; all are come to pass unto you, and not one thing hath failed thereof (Joshua 23:14).

Then the covenant was renewed.

> And the people served the Lord all the days of Joshua, and all the days of the elders that outlived Joshua (Judges 2:7).

The era of the judges

After the conquest of Canaan was complete, Israel entered the period of the judges, and what a different story it was. This era is a continual cycle of sinning, oppression, deliverance; sinning, oppression, deliverance. "There arose another generation after them, which knew not the Lord" (Judges 2:10). "Every man did that which was right in his own eyes" (Judges 17:6).

Judgment upon the heathen

Israel was instructed to destroy the heathen places of

worship and drive the oppressing nations from the land. Archaeology has helped us to understand the deplorable state of the nations and why God would have so judged them.

At Byblos, twenty-five miles north of Beirut, excavations have uncovered great open-air sanctuaries with their heathen altars and sun pillars. Before Israel's conquest of Canaan, the land was filled with pagan temples and altars. Immoral, sensual rites were performed and human sacrifices offered.

The Canaanites and the surrounding nations were saturated with idolatry and immorality and had passed their day of probation. At other times, God used nations such as Assyria and Babylon to bring His judgment upon other nations. And now He used Israel as His rod of anger against the idolatrous nations of Canaan.

At Megiddo, archaeologists have uncovered the largest Canaanite altar yet discovered in Palestine. Standing higher than a man, the round altar, thirty feet in diameter, rests in a vast sacred complex. Also found was a beautiful limestone altar with horns, like altars used by the children of Israel (see 1 Kings 1:50).

Excavations at Hazor and Gezer have also produced their Canaanite altars and sun pillars. On June 26, 1990, a small calf idol four and a half inches long was found during the excavations of the Philistine city of Askelon.

The excavations at Ras Shamrah, the ancient Ugarit in north Syria, have disclosed the most telling evidence of the degraded and corrupt condition of the Canaanites. In 1975, I visited Ras Shamrah and observed the extensive work carried on under the direction of the French archaeologist, Dr. Claude Shaeffer.

Diggings there began in 1929 and continued until the outbreak of World War II. They were then resumed in 1950. The later work revealed a massive palace covering ten thousand square yards.

The city of Ugarit had boasted a number of temples, three of which were excavated. Two of them were dedicated respectively to the gods Dagan and Baal.

Of prime importance was the library found in the high priest's house that stood between the two temples. It contained hundreds of tablets inscribed with various languages. Small tablets may seem very insignificant, but to archaeologists and scholars they have proven far more valuable than the awesome remains that dazzle the tourists.

Studying the tablets, scholars discovered that the greater portion of them were in an unknown script, a script that later proved to be alphabetic in nature. The new language became known as Ugaritic. The alphabetic script later developed into the Phoenician script from which the English alphabet is derived.

Until his death in 1982, Dr. Mitchell Dahood stood out as the world's foremost authority on the Ugaritic texts. At a lecture in Washington, D.C., I listened as he related numerous examples of how the Ugaritic text has enabled scholars to translate correctly words in our Bible that previously had been unclear.

The Ras Shamrah diggings uncovered many mythological texts. Of particular interest were those relating to Baal, the chief weather god of the Canaanites—the god of the storms. Although supposedly in control of the weather, the prophets of Baal were incapable of bringing rain at the time of their notable contest with Elijah on Mount Carmel.

Among the images found at Ras Shamrah were those of Astarte, the Ishtar of the monuments of Assyria and Babylonia, the goddess of love and fertility, the Queen of Heaven, from whom the term *Easter* is derived. The finds at Ras Shamrah have contributed substantially to understanding the base immorality of the Canaanite culture, with its temples of prostitution, and to an understanding of why God willed the destruction of the Canaanites.

Early in the period of the Judges, Israel was attacked by the Canaanites, who streamed in from the northwest through the Valley of Esdraelon. There the Canaanites suffered a disastrous defeat under Deborah and Barak, and forty years of peace followed.

Then came seven years of oppression by the Midianites, followed by their defeat under Gideon and his small band of three hundred. Gideon's band slaughtered the Midianites as they swarmed in from the east through this same historic Valley of Esdraelon. And again Israel had rest for forty years.

The Philistines

Israel's greatest enemies were the Philistines. Their first appearance in secular history comes from inscriptions on the walls of the mortuary temple of Rameses III in Egypt. Since they came from the Phoenician coast, they are called "Sea Peoples." They had invaded Egypt from the north through Syria and Palestine. The inscription records how, during the eighth year of Rameses III's reign (1190 B.C.), he drove them from the land.

After being driven from Egypt, they settled in five coastal cities in southern Palestine—Gaza, Askelon, Ashdod, Ekron, and Gath. Their impact on the land is suggested by the name Palestine, which they gave to the area.

The Philistines' first encounter with Israel came in the days of Samson because of their encroachment upon the territories of Dan and Judah. The tribe of Dan was subdued by the Philistines and forced to resettle in the north.

While engaged in excavations at Gezer, I became well acquainted with the area in which Samson carried on his antics. Each morning our drive from Jerusalem to the dig would take us down the western slopes of the Judean ridge into the Shafelah, or Lowlands. Emerging from the mountains just below Kirjath-jearim, we entered the Valley of Sorek. There Samson's Inn, a restaurant and way station, stands as a ready reminder of the historic past. Also, not far away, the smoke ascends from Samson's Cement Factory. Bethshemesh lay at the foot of the hills to the south.

From the valley of Sorek, Samson went eastward to Askelon,

where he slew thirty men and caught three hundred foxes, tied their tails together, and put them afire in a wheat field. He also slew a thousand Philistines with the jawbone of an ass. All together, he judged Israel for twenty years.

Samson's demise came because of his love for Delilah, who lived in this valley. Finally, in the hands of the Philistines who put out his eyes, he was bound and taken to Gaza, where he ground grain in the prison house.

His life ended when, with his great strength returned, he took hold of the pillars of the temple of Dagon, bringing it down upon himself and the three thousand assembled within (see Judges 13-16).

In the days of Samuel, the Philistines attacked and defeated Israel in the Valley of Aphek, a few miles north and east of present-day Tel Aviv. Israel thought that with the ark of the covenant in their ranks things would go differently, so they had it brought from the tabernacle at Shiloh. Again they were defeated, suffering thirty thousand casualties. The ark was taken, and Eli's two sons were slain. Eli, the priest, while officiating at the tabernacle, fell over dead upon receiving word of the disaster.

Following their great victory, the Philistines took the ark to Ashdod, a site that has been under excavation since 1962. In 1965, I heard an illustrated lecture in Jerusalem by Dr. M. Dothan, director of the Ashdod dig. He reported on his work there, which includes the discovery of the remains of the Temple of Dagon referred to in the Scriptures (see 1 Samuel 5:2-5).

Excavators at Ashdod also found the debris caused by the destruction during the invasion of Sargon, referred to in Isaiah 20:1. They also found a memorial stone in broken condition set up to commemorate the victory.

According to the biblical account, the presence of the ark brought disaster to Ashdod, even causing their god in the Temple of Dagon to topple over and break. The ark was then sent to Gaza, and then to Ekron.

Ekron is the last of the Philistine cities to be excavated.[7] During a visit there in October of 1987, I saw the work then under way. Ekron was once a highly fortified city of more than fifty acres, one of the largest cities of Palestine and a chief industrial city. Its largest industry was the production of olive oil, accomplished on a massive scale; some one hundred large oil presses have been discovered.[8]

Ekron was conquered by Sargon, Sennacherib, and probably by Nebuchadnezzar, who seems to have brought its olive-oil business to an end.

At Ekron, the presence of the ark of the testament also brought misfortune, so it was put on a bullock cart and sent back to the Israelites at Bethshemesh, the nearest city of the Levites. The bullocks pulling the cart halted in the field of Sorek, where the ark was retrieved. A yellow marker recounting these events stands in that field today.

The Israelites took the ark up the mountain to Kirjath-jearim, a short distance away. From here, King David would some years later have it transported to Jerusalem.

Through the centuries, Kirjath-jearim was an important stop for pilgrims on their way to Jerusalem to visit the holy places. On the distant hills about nine miles away, they would get their first glimpse of the holy city, then fall to their knees and kiss the ground. Today the site, crowned with the remains of a Crusader castle, is another of Israel's national parks and resort centers.

After twenty years of Philistine oppression, Samuel called Israel to meet with him at Ebenezer, near the site of the crushing defeat so many years before. There he called them to repent and turn to the Lord. They fasted all that day, confessing their sins. As a result, God blessed them with a great revival.

At the time, the Philistines were again encamped at Aphek. Thinking Israel had gathered for a council of war, they launched another attack. The battle waged on the same field of Israel's earlier defeat, only this time the tables were turned, and God gave Israel a decisive victory. The Philistines were forced to return to Israel many of the strongholds they had occupied, and they were restrained from acts of hostility for many years to come.

> And the cities which the Philistines had taken from Israel were restored to Israel, from Ekron even unto Gath; and the coasts thereof did Israel deliver out of the hands of the Philistines. And there was peace between Israel and the Amorites. And Samuel judged Israel all the days of his life (1 Samuel 7:14, 15).

Samuel was the last of the judges. Soon Israel would ask for a king. This brings us to the period of kings Saul, David, and Solomon—Israel's Golden Age.

---

1. Bryant G. Wood, "Did the Israelites Conquer Jericho? A New Look at the Archaeological Evidence," *BAR*, March/April 1990, 44-57.

2. Ibid., 57.

3. Piotr Bienkowski, "Jericho Was Destroyed in the Middle Bronze Age, Not the Late Bronze Age"; Bryant G. Wood, "Dating Jericho's Destruction: Bienkowski Is Wrong on All Counts," *BAR*, September/October 1990, 45-49, 68.

4. "Hershel Shanks replies to Dever," ibid., 18.

5. Adam Zertal, "Has Joshua's Altar Been Found on Mt. Ebal?" *BAR*, January/February 1985, 26-43. See also "Joshua and the Archeologist," *Reader's Digest*, September 1990, 135ff.

6. Asher S. Kaufman, "Fixing the Site of the Tabernacle at Shiloh," *BAR*, November/December 1988, 46-52.

7. The site of Gath has not been determined, nor the exact location of the ancient Gaza.

8. Trude Dothan and Seymour Gitin, "Ekron of the Philistines," *BAR*, January/February 1990, 20-25; Seymour Gitin, "Ekron of the Philistines," part 2, *BAR*, March/April 1990. See also: Trude Dothan, "What We Know About the Philistines," *BAR*, July/August 1982, 20-44.

Chapter 14

Israel's Golden Age

A bout six miles north of Jerusalem is the mound of the ancient city of Ramah, the home of Samuel. From here this noble prophet judged Israel for twenty years. Assisting him in the affairs of government were his two sons. But his sons became corrupt, accepted bribes, and perverted judgment.

Meanwhile, the Philistines, centered in their five coastal cities, became increasingly oppressive. These conditions led to Israel's demand for a king, and Saul was their first leader.

Shortly after Saul's coronation, his son Jonathan routed the Philistines at Michmash, about four miles north of Ramah. Then David, the youthful shepherd boy, slew Goliath in the Valley of Elah.

Because of Saul's unfaithfulness, David was selected by God to succeed him to the throne. Meanwhile, David's life was constantly threatened by the jealous king. To find refuge, he sought out the shelter of the Palestinian caves.

I once joined a party exploring the caves in the lowlands between Hebron and the sea. There, in a remote and desolate area, we came across huge caverns among the colorful limestone cliffs, caverns large enough to accommodate hundreds of men. One of them might have been the cave of Adullum, where David hid from King Saul (see 1 Samuel 22:1, 2).

David also found a hiding place in the caves of En Gedi. Today, En Gedi is a lovely resort area about halfway down the

140

western side of the Dead Sea. This oasis is fed by beautiful springs. A foaming waterfall forms a pool that bathers find refreshing. The surrounding hills are clustered with caves. In these caves, Yigael Yadin discovered scrolls similar to those found in the Dead Sea caves. These scrolls, however, were hidden at a later time during the Jewish Bar Kochba revolt against the Romans in the early second century A.D. They include actual dispatches sent out by Bar Kochba, the Judean chief.

It was in these caves that David and his six hundred men found a refuge. Saul, searching for David with three thousand troops, went to sleep near the mouth of the cave in which David was hiding. The fearless but compassionate David cut off a part of Saul's skirt, but spared the king's life (see 1 Samuel 23:29; 24:1-4).

Saul's palace stood at Gibeah, two miles north of Jerusalem, and a quarter or fifth of a mile off the main highway to the right. The palace remains have been excavated; however, the crown of the hill is now dominated by the unfinished palace of King Hussein of the Hashemite Kingdom of Jordan. From this lofty perch, King Saul ruled Israel for forty years.

Saul's Waterloo finally came in a battle against the Philistines at Mount Gilboa, in which he was mortally wounded. When his soldiers refused to thrust him through with a spear, he assumed the task himself, thus ending his life.

The Scripture states that the Philistines, to show off their trophies, "put his armour in the house of Ashtaroth: and they fastened his body to the wall of Beth-shan" (1 Samuel 31:10).

Beth-shan stood to the west at a pass going down into the Jordan Valley. The ancient city was excavated in a lengthy expedition from the University of Pennsylvania museum that continued from 1921 to 1933. A visit there reveals the large theater that was exposed.

More significantly, two temples were uncovered. One temple was dedicated to the female goddess, Ashtaroth. It is the very temple in which Saul's armor was placed. The other temple was dedicated to the male god Dagon. The temples were next to each other, connected by a complex of rooms and store-houses.

The pool of Gibeon

The conspicuous mound of Gibeon, the home of the Gibeonites, is six miles northwest of Jerusalem. The tabernacle was moved to this site after the destruction of Shiloh by the Philistines, and it stood here during the reigns of David and Solomon before the temple was built.

The site was excavated from 1956 to 1962 by the prominent scholar and archaeologist, James B. Pritchard, of the University of Pennsylvania. Excavators found the very pool mentioned in the Bible where Abner and the servants of Ishbosheth, the son of Saul, fought against Joab, the servant of David (see 2 Samuel 2:13-17). Of their gathering at the pool we read:

[They] went out, and met together by the pool of Gibeon: and they sat down, the one on the one side of the pool, and the other on the other side of the pool (verse 13).

There they chose twelve men for each side, all of whom seem to have perished (verse 16). However, in the day's battle that followed, "Abinar was beaten" (verse 17).

I visited Gibeon when the pool was being excavated. It is thirty-six feet across and thirty-six feet deep, with steps leading down to the bottom. Just the day before my visit, excavators found a jar handle in the pool with the name *Gibeon* inscribed on it. A picture of the jar handle appeared in the next issue of *Time* magazine, along with a report about the dig. It is somewhat rare to find an artifact with the name of the site inscribed on it, which positively identifies the site.

Midway between Jerusalem and Beer-sheba, on the highest point of the Judean ridge, stands the city of Hebron. Upon the death of Saul, God directed David to this city, and from here he ruled as king for seven years.

The city of David

Jerusalem now enters the picture for the first time in the story of Israel. As the site chosen by David for his capital, the city, then a Jebusite fortress, occupied a central and elevated position. It was well protected by the surrounding mountains.

The choice of this Jebusite fortress, which is south of the present temple mount, was no doubt influenced primarily by the fact that the Gihon spring flows at its feet, furnishing a rich supply of water.

The Jebusite fortress where David built the original city of Jerusalem is today known as Ophel. The site was excavated by Yigal Shiloh from 1978 until his death on November 14, 1987.

From the spring at Gihon, the water runs through a tunnel into the pool of Gihon, which was outside the walls of the city of Jerusalem in David's day. About twenty-five feet inside the tunnel, a shaft rises to the surface above, which was inside the city. It was through this shaft that David's men entered and took the city from the Jebusites in a sneak attack. The account reads, "And David said on that day, Whosoever getteth up to the gutter, and smiteth the Jebusites . . . shall be chief and captain" (2 Samuel 5:8).

Joab responded to the challenge; went up the gutter, or shaft; and thus gained entrance into the city and took the fortress. From above, the shaft is reached by way of a lengthy tunnel. Both the tunnel and shaft have been cleared in recent years and are open to the public. On my visit in 1987, I saw the spot where one of the engineers working on the job had demonstrated the feasibility of Joab's ascent by climbing up the shaft just like David's valiant servant once did.[1]

The purpose of the shaft was to provide access to the water supply in times of siege, the Gihon spring being outside the city wall. The shaft is now known as Warren's Shaft in recognition of Charles Warren, who first discovered it more than a hundred years ago.

From the Gihon spring, we followed a path up the hill to

the site where archaeologists have been at work. About seventy-five feet above the spring, parts of the Jebusite wall have been exposed. Approaching the top, one stands amazed before the stepped-stone ramparts that supported this ancient citadel of David and later supported the palace and administrative buildings of Solomon. Other remains include a tower of the first century A.D. and a house destroyed in the general destruction that came to the city under Nebuchadnezzar, the Babylonian king.

Solomon leveled off the mountain opposite the city, developing the platform upon which the temple was erected. His palace and administrative buildings were constructed between the temple and David's city. The monumental stepped-stone structure beneath this entire complex rises taller than a five-story building.[2]

David's seven-year rule in Hebron was followed by thirty-three years in Jerusalem. His reign was one of conquest, and the borders of the kingdom were greatly enlarged. The early period was marked by a battle against the Philistines in the Valley of Rephaim to the west of the capital city. But David

> smote the host of the Philistines from Gibeon even to Gazer. And the fame of David went out into all lands; and the Lord brought the fear of him upon all nations (1 Chronicles 14:16, 17).

The sacred ark had been deposited in a home at Kirjath-jearim after its return from the Philistines. Now, under King David, a grand procession transported it up the Judean hills to Jerusalem, nine miles distant. The old road they would have followed is still visible—considerably different from the superhighway of today.

As the triumphal procession approached the city, the singers demanded: "Lift up your heads, O ye gates ... and the King of Glory shall come in" (Psalm 24:7).

The gates were opened wide, and the sacred ark, which

housed God's holy law, was taken into the city and deposited in the tent prepared for it.

Critics once claimed that the psalms attributed to David could not have been written as early as 1000 B.C. But in more recent years, many similar writings dating to that period have been found. David was indeed the sweet singer of Israel.

The splendors of Solomon

While David's reign was one of conquest, Solomon did more to promote the culture of the nation. Solomon's temple was perhaps the most beautiful building the world has ever seen.

A view of Jerusalem from the slopes of the Mount of Olives offers a splendid panorama of the mountain the temple was built on. The Dome of the Rock now occupies the central position where the temple once stood.

A walk within the temple would have dazzled the beholder, for the walls, ceilings, and even the floors were all covered with gold (see 1 Kings 6:20-22, 30; 2 Chronicles 3:4-7). King Solomon also had two hundred large shields of gold and three hundred smaller ones. His throne was made of ivory and overlaid with fine gold. The goblets and household articles were all of gold (see 1 Kings 10:16-18, 21).

Consider the weight of all this gold. Solomon's shields weighed about four thousand pounds, or more than two tons.

The queen of Sheba presented Solomon with a gift of four and a half tons of gold (1 Kings 10:10). This may seem a fantastic exaggeration. However, the Assyrian king Tiglath-pileser III received a similar amount when he conquered the city of Tyre in 730 B.C. And Sargon II gave as large a gift to the gods of Babylon from the booty received on his Babylonian campaign. In Egypt, Thutmose III presented to the temple at Karnak a gift of gold amounting to thirteen and a half tons.[3]

What happened to all the gold of Solomon's temple and palace?

And it came to pass in the fifth year of king Rehoboam,

that Shishak king of Egypt came up against Jerusalem:
And he took away the treasures of the house of the Lord,
and the treasures of the king's house; he even took away
all: and he took away all the shields of gold which
Solomon had made (1 Kings 14:25, 26).

What did Shishak do with all this gold? He died within a
year or so of this campaign and was succeeded by his son,
Osorkon I. Directly after Shishak's death, and within ten
years of Solomon's death, Osorkon recorded his lavish gifts to
the gods and goddesses of Egypt—gifts that included at least
383 tons of silver and gold.[4] Apparently Solomon's gold ended
up as a gift to the Egyptian gods.

Walking on the temple mount of Jerusalem today, on the
western side, one first enters a beautiful colonnade. Before
1965, it led to a door with steps descending to a boxed-in alley
several feet below. The area, about twenty feet wide and sixty
feet long, ran along the ancient western wall, known for
centuries as the Wailing Wall. Here pious Jews would come to
wail the loss of the temple, when international conditions
would permit.

A visit to the site today reveals a remarkable change. One
of the first acts of the Jews following the Six-Day War of June
1967 was to clear the area fronting the wall. It is now a large
plaza, used for religious gatherings and national celebrations.
But the Jewish pilgrims still come to the wall to pray—the
men on the left of a barrier, and the women on the right.

King Herod, in preparation for rebuilding the temple,
doubled the size of the platform. Viewing the lower portion of
the eastern wall, a break is seen where a seam indicates a
different time of construction. The work to the south of the
seam represents Herod's addition. The massive stones to the
right of the seam are believed by the archaeologists who have
labored there to represent the work of King Solomon.[5]

Among the seven gates piercing the walled city of Jerusalem, the Golden Gate was the most auspicious. It offered the

most direct approach to the temple mount from the Kidron Valley and the Mount of Olives, although entrance through it has been barred for centuries.

In recent years, while digging in the area fronting this monumental gateway, a team of archaeologists uncovered an earlier gateway. They suggest that this could possibly be the work of Solomon. The masonry of the eastern wall, previously referred to, and that of this Solomonic gateway are the same. The dating of this masonry, however, is still being debated.

Since the gate adjoins a Muslim cemetery, the area has been restored to its former appearance so that none of the gateway is visible today.[6]

Nehemiah 3:15 speaks of the "king's garden." Walking southward from the temple area toward the Kidron Valley, one comes upon the ancient well of Ein Rogel. It was at this well that Adonijah gathered his brothers and David's officers in an effort to seize the kingdom after the death of his father David. Also known as Job's Well, it is 125 feet deep and still in use today. The garden area around the well, like much of Jerusalem, has changed considerably since it has come under Jewish control.

By developing extensive trade routes, Solomon enriched the kingdom. He commanded a Red Sea fleet, built and manned by Phoenicians. A principal port of call was Tarshish, in southern Spain, near Gibraltar. They sailed out of the port at Ezion Geber, one of the largest ports of Solomon's day, making round trips once every three years to fabled Ophir (see 1 Kings 9:26-28; 10:11, 22; 22:48; 2 Chronicles 20:36, 37). Solomon also, as a middleman, dealt in chariots and horses and had a monopoly on imports and exports.

Recent explorations in Sinai and the Negev have uncovered what are believed to have been fortresses established by Solomon.[7] He may have built the initial fortress at Arad, several miles east of Beer-sheba. At Arad he built a temple, patterned after that of Jerusalem, but it was used for a mixture of true worship with that of the gods of the nations. Excavations indicate that it was probably destroyed at the time of the great revival that came to Judah in the days of Josiah.[8]

The Bible as an archaeological guide

In 1 Kings 9:15, we read of Solomon's building enterprises:

> This is the reason of the levy which king Solomon raised; for to build the house of the Lord, and his own house, and Millo, and the wall of Jerusalem, and Hazor, and Megiddo, and Gezer.

The cities of Hazor, Megiddo, and Gezer stood at strategic locations—Hazor guarded the approach from the north, Megiddo guarded the route through the famed Megiddo pass, and Gezer guarded the way from the south. All three of these cities have been excavated, with very fascinating results.

The mound of Megiddo has felt the spade intermittently over a period of many years, beginning in 1903. Today, it is a large, open-air museum and a favorite tourist attraction. Entry to the Solomonic city was by way of an impressive double-entry gateway, now clearly discernible.

Walking onto the mound, one sees the casemate walls that surrounded the thirteen-acre city. Casemate was a type of construction used by Solomon, consisting of parallel walls with partitions between.

Signs along a well-marked path identify the areas where the residences of the provisional governor and military commandant once stood, and where, until recent years, it was believed the king had his stables.

The path also leads to the unique water system, though dated to Ahab of the ninth century. Steps lead down to a shaft 120 feet deep. Forty-two more winding steps down the shaft lead to a tunnel 300 feet in length. This brings us at last to the spring, which was located outside the city wall. The approach through the tunnel provided access from within the city in times of siege.

Yadin digs at Hazor

Hazor, about eight miles north of the Sea of Galilee, presented a particular challenge to Dr. Yigael Yadin. As a student of archaeology, he was impressed with the size of this mound. Its lower city covers twenty-five acres and its upper city covers fifteen acres. The frequent reference to Hazor, both in the Bible and in nonbiblical texts, also fascinated Dr. Yadin. And he hoped that some day he would have the opportunity to dig at Hazor.

During the War of Independence, as he often passed the site of Hazor, his hopes were renewed. In 1952, he resigned as an officer in the army and went to London, where he studied for two years on his doctoral degree. While there he determined to start a large-scale excavation of the mound.

The results of his dig, which ran from 1955 to 1958, are graphically reported in his volume, *Hazor: The Rediscovery of a Great Citadel of the Bible*.[9] In regard to this project, Yadin wrote:

> Some of what I am about to relate may sound like a detective story, but the truth is that our great guide was the Bible; and as an archaeologist I cannot imagine a greater thrill than working with the Bible in one hand and the spade in the other. This was the true secret of our discoveries of the Solomonic period.[10]

As Yadin uncovered the stables of Hazor, he found them to be similar to those at Megiddo. But at Hazor, they joined onto walls dating to the later period of King Ahab. Then, digging beneath the structures of Ahab, Yadin and his helpers uncovered the remains of the palace of Solomon. Ahab had built the stables on top of the ruins of Solomon's palace. This led Yadin back to Megiddo in 1960. Sure enough, the so-called "stables of Solomon" were not his at all, but those belonging to Ahab, the Israelite king.

Also at Megiddo, Yadin carefully examined the design of

Solomon's gateway, taking a copy of the plans with him to Hazor. He reasoned that if Solomon had constructed the gateway at Hazor, it would probably be similar to that of Megiddo. So he laid it out on the bare ground, instructing a workman, "You dig there," to another, "You dig there," and to still another, "You dig there." More than that, he told them exactly what they could expect to find.

To their utter amazement, here at Hazor they found just what Yadin had predicted—a gateway exactly like Solomon's gateway at Megiddo. The workmen thought surely Yadin must be a wizard. Then he explained to them how he had calculated it all.

Reporting on this, he says:

> When our 'prophecies' proved correct, our prestige went up tremendously, and we were regarded as wizards. . . . When we read them [the workmen] the biblical verse about Solomon's activities in Hazor, Meggido and Gezer [1 Kings 9:15], our prestige took a dive, but that of the Bible rose sky-high![11]

Checking out the Bible at Gezer

But what about Gezer? The mound covers thirty acres, as compared to the twenty-five of Hazor and the thirteen of Megiddo. The site was first excavated in 1902 by Macalister. Excavations were resumed in 1964 and continued through 1973.

I participated in this dig during the summer of 1965, working under the direction of Dr. G. Ernest Wright. He worked quite differently from Macalister. Macalister was the sole supervisor with two hundred Arab workmen to look after. There were about twenty-five of us, working in teams of five each, with a supervisor over each group. My group consisted of a professor from General Theological Seminary in New York, a Baptist layman, a Catholic priest, a Jewish student, and myself, a Seventh-day Adventist minister. Our supervisor was Dr. James Ross, a Presbyterian minister and a professor at Drew University. So ours was quite an ecumenical undertaking, and we enjoyed the very best of relations.

Each group worked in an area about fifteen feet square. Early in the dig, we came across outcrops of rock that would prove to be a part of the casemate wall of Solomon. The tools used were mostly the small garden variety, and the work proceeded with greatest care, lest we destroy some important object. Dr. Wright cautioned us that the week before, a man with a pick had accidentally destroyed a fine pottery jar.

As the digging progressed, all pieces of pottery were placed in red buckets and labeled with the location where they were found. The dirt was put into black buckets made of old tires and wheeled to the dump.

The pottery was washed in a large tub beneath a canopy, then laid out to dry. Later, Dr. Wright would sort through the pottery, choose specimens for further evaluation, and discard the rest.

Pottery is the key to determining the period and the culture of the site being exposed, for each period and people has its own characteristic style. Dr. Wright, one of the world's foremost authorities on pottery dating, could "read" the pieces at a glance.

What about the gateway at Gezer? Near the square I was working in were the remains of what Macalister had identified as a Maccabean castle. Dr. Yadin proposed that the castle was in fact the Solomonic gateway. One of the principal purposes of the dig was to check out Yadin's theory. Would the Gezer gateway match up with those of Megiddo and Hazor? Yadin quotes the conclusion from Dr. William G. Dever, who later supervised, and later reported on, the dig:

> The sealed pottery from the floors and the makeup below was characteristic red-burnished ware of the late tenth century BC. Solomon did indeed re-build Gezer![12]

Referring to his key text, 1 Kings 9:15, which states that Solomon rebuilt the three cities, Yadin writes:

> Hardly ever in the history of archaeological digging has such a short verse in the Bible helped so much in identifying and dating actual remains found by the spade.[13]

In recent years, however, certain scholars have challenged these conclusions and have tried to convince the archaeological community that the work at Gezer, particularly the so-called Solomonic gate, was built in later years by King Ahab.

The matter was settled in the summer of 1990 when Dever teamed up with Prof. Randal Younker, director of the Institute of Archaeology, Horn Archaeological Museum, Andrews University, for a return dig at Gezer. Additional convincing evidence was uncovered so that today the six-chambered gate at Gezer can more confidently than ever be called a Solomonic gate. Archaeology has again demonstrated in a remarkable way the reliability of the Bible.

---

1. Yigal Shiloh, "The Rediscovery of Warren's Shaft," *BAR*, July/August 1981, 24-39.

2. Hershel Shanks, "The City of David After Five Years of Digging," *BAR*, November/December 1985, 22-38.

3. Alan R. Millard, "Does the Bible Exaggerate King Solomon's Golden Wealth?" *BAR*, May/June 1989, 20-34.

4. Kenneth A. Kitchen, "Where Did Solomon's Gold Go?" *BAR*, May/June 1989, 30.

5. Ernest-Marie Laperrousaz, "King Solomon's Wall Still Supports the Temple Mount," *BAR*, May/June 1987, 34-44.

6. James Fleming, "The Undiscovered Gate Beneath Jerusalem's Golden Gate," *BAR*, January/February 1983, 24-37.

7. Rudolph Cohen, "The Fortresses King Solomon Built to Protect His Southern Border," *BAR*, May/June 1985, 56-70.

8. Ze'Ev Herzog, Miriam Aharoni, Anson F. Rainey, "Arad: An Ancient Israelite Fortress with a Temple to Yahweh," *BAR*, March/April 1987, 16-35.

9. Yigael Yadin, *Hazor: The Rediscovery of a Great Citadel of the Bible* (New York: Random House, 1975).

10. Ibid., 187.

11. Ibid., 193, 195.

12. Ibid., 203.

13. Ibid., 205.

Chapter 15

The Divided Empire

The kingdom of David and Solomon extended from the Red Sea in the south to the Euphrates River in the north. The reign of David and Solomon was the age of the Golden Empire, when Israel came nearest to reaching God's purposes for her as a nation.

From Jerusalem Solomon guided the destiny of Israel, but unfortunately, prosperity led to his self-exaltation and his disregard for God's commands. He married foreign wives, and through them he and the nation were led to worship foreign gods. Heathen altars, high places, and temples soon dotted the landscape. Heavy taxes were levied to support Solomon's grand building enterprises, leading the nation to the verge of bankruptcy.

But God's unfailing love finally drew Solomon back. Repenting of his gross sins, he returned to the Lord with all his fervor. He recorded his futile search for happiness apart from God, along with important lessons for all humankind. We cherish the books he wrote: Proverbs, Ecclesiastes, and the Song of Solomon.

Despite his sincere repentance, his evil past brought inevitable consequences. On his death his son, Rehoboam, came to Shechem to be received as king by all the tribes. They requested the new king to lessen their burdens. He vowed, instead, to increase them. There was an open break, and the kingdom was divided. As a result, Jeroboam ruled the northern tribes from Shechem, and Rehoboam continued to rule the southern tribes from Jerusalem.

At Jerusalem, Rehoboam started to reign on a right course. "For three years they walked in the way of David and Solomon" (2 Chronicles 11:17). However:

> It came to pass, when Rehoboam had established the kingdom, and had strengthened himself, he forsook the law of the Lord, and all Israel with him (2 Chronicles 12:1).

> For they also built them high places, and images [pillars], and groves, on every high hill, and under every green tree (1 Kings 14:23).

Shishak plunders Jerusalem

Because of their apostasy, God permitted enemies to come against Judah, as the southern kingdom was called.

> And it came to pass in the fifth year of king Rehoboam, that Shishak king of Egypt came up against Jerusalem: And he took away the treasures of the house of the Lord, and the treasures of the king's house; he even took away all (1 Kings 14:25, 26).

Shishak's campaign against Jerusalem was the first of twenty sieges the capital city would experience. Five times it would be destroyed.

On the outside of the southern wall of the great temple of Amon at Karnak, a relief pictures Shishak's triumphal campaign against Judah. This devastating expedition left 150 cities plundered or destroyed, each represented by the head of a captive from each city being inscribed on the wall.

Among the cities named by Shishak was Gezer. While digging there, Dr. G. Ernest Wright, standing in a trench that had been opened, directed our attention to what he believed to be the debris caused by the destruction of that memorable campaign. It is a great thrill to see firsthand the evidence of events recorded in the Bible.

With the archaeologists at Bethel and Dan

While Rehoboam was facing his problems in Jerusalem, Jeroboam was doing what he could to assure the northern tribes' loyalty to him. To this end he set up centers of worship at Bethel and Dan.

Bethel first felt the archaeologists' spade in 1934 in an expedition under the direction of Dr. William Albright, assisted by Dr. James Kelso. Dr. Kelso, of Pittsburgh Theological Seminary, continued as the director of the project with further digs in 1954, 1957, and 1960.

The Kelso Bible Lands Museum in the Pittsburgh seminary features his work. Many articles from Bethel are on display, some from the period of Jeroboam.

A visit to Dan takes us to the far north near the present Lebanese border. This city, which marked the northern border of Israel, rested near the foot of Mount Hermon, where a natural spring gushes from underground. The spring is the source of one of the four small streams that unite and become the Jordan River.

At Dan, as at Bethel, Jeroboam set up a "high place" for worship. In the summer of 1979 archaeologist Avraham Biran, digging at Dan, discovered a huge, mud-brick gateway, dating back to about 1900-1700 B.C., probably earlier than 1700. Consisting of two towers joined by a massive arch, it proved to be the only such gateway in the Near East ever to be found still intact. A platform, probably the throne of Israel's king, was also found within a ninth century–B.C. Israelite gate. Socketed bases suggest that posts were inserted in the holes to support a canopy over the throne. A paved royal ceremonial road led up to the gate.

Further excavations in the area uncovered a huge "high place" believed to be that built by Jeroboam to compete with the temple worship of Jerusalem (1 Kings 12:29). The original high place measured approximately twenty-two feet by sixty feet. This structure was destroyed by fire and rebuilt in the ninth century B.C. to a size of sixty by sixty-two feet. A horned incense altar which may also date to this period was discovered in an adjacent courtyard. This high place was rebuilt a third time in the first half of the eighth century B.C., at which time a twenty-seven-foot-wide monumental stairway was built against it. The high place apparently continued in use until Israel's captivity in 724 B.C.[*]

The Omri-Ahab dynasty

Omri, the Israelite king who came to the throne thirty-five years after the death of Jeroboam, founded a new dynasty at Shechem. Later he moved the capital to Tirzah, and then to the crest of the hill at Samaria. The conspicuous mound of Samaria rises four hundred feet above the valley, seven miles northeast of Shechem. With its formidable defensive position, Samaria would remain the capital of the northern kingdom until its capture by the Assyrians.

The crest of the hill at Samaria is approached today by way of a Roman road, flanked by its characteristic columns. On the summit, archaeologists have exposed a Roman theater and the palace and temple of Emperor Augustus (27 B.C.-A.D. 14). The diggings have also uncovered the palace of Omri, built on bedrock, in confirmation of the scripture that states that Omri was the first to build at Samaria.

Omri was a man of conquest. According to 2 Kings 3:4, 5, Mesha, king of Moab, was forced to pay tribute to him. This verse of Scripture is confirmed on the famous Moabite Stone on which "Omri the Israelite" is named as the oppressor of Moab. Discovered at Dibon in Moab in 1868, the stone, now in the Louvre in Paris, stands four feet high and is inscribed with thirty-two lines. On the stone, Mesha states that it was set up "to commemorate my deliverance from Israel." This text also proves that Mesha was not a fictitious character. Assyrian texts have also been found that mention Omri.

Omri is the first Hebrew king whose name was found in nonbiblical records. Since the discovery of the Moabite Stone, the names of eleven other Hebrew kings have come to light. All together, the ancient texts have produced the names of seven kings of Israel and five kings of Judah. The last one, Jehoash, was found on an Assyrian inscription in Iraq in 1967. This testimony from the ancient texts is amazing, considering that critical scholars once questioned the existence of some of the Hebrew kings.

The excavations of Samaria have also produced the remains of the palace of Ahab, who succeeded Omri to the throne. The prophet Amos of that day thundered against Ahab's luxurious living on beds of ivory (see Amos 3:15; 6:4). Significantly, the king's palace has been among the few places in Israel where ivory articles have been found, another instance of archaeology confirming the accurate details of the biblical accounts.

The worship of Baal

Ahab married the Phoenician princess, Jezebel, who in turn led Israel into the worship of Baal. The high places of Baal with their temples, altars, and sun pillars have been uncovered at such places as Byblos, Ras Shamrah, and Gezer.

As a daughter of the king, Jezebel would have served as a priestess in the temple of Baal. The most impressive monuments to Baal worship to be seen today are the grandiose temples of Baalbek in Lebanon—the area inhabited by the ancient Phoenicians.

Baalbek is known to be one of the oldest cities in the world. The city was originally called *Baal-Beqa*, or "city of Baal," but in the days of the Greeks and Romans it was called *Heliopolis*, the "city of the sun." Although the visible remains at Baalbek are of Roman origin, it is not unlikely that here stood the ancient Phoenician Baal temple in which Jezebel ministered.

A visit to Baalbek is a memorable experience. A monumental staircase leads to the sacred enclave with its immense temple chambers and courts. The Court of the Sacrifice is 221 feet in diameter and contains a gigantic altar.

The Temple of Jupiter at Baalbek is surrounded with columns sixty-six feet high—as high as a six-story building—and seven feet thick. The colossal foundation stones are up to sixty feet long. One of them remains in the quarry because of a flaw. It is sixty-four feet long, fourteen feet across, and weighs fourteen hundred tons. Three foundation stones about the same size are in place in the foundation of the temple structure.

The temple of Bacchus is a part of the same temple complex. It is decorated with portraits of Roman gods and emblems of life and death. Twenty-four of the original fifty columns, fifty-seven feet tall, are still in place.

The thunderings of Elijah

East of the Jordan lived the righteous man Elijah. His prayers for revival and reformation in Israel were interrupted by God. God commanded him to deliver the message to King Ahab, "There shall not be dew nor rain these years, but according to my word" (1 Kings 17:1).

Three and one-half years of drought followed. Elijah survived, first at the Brook Cherith, and then in a Phoenician widow's home at Zarephath—today's Sarepta, a coastal town between Tyre and Sidon.

The drought ended with Elijah's confrontation with the prophets of Baal and the prophets of Asherah on Mount Carmel. Carmel is a mountain range about twenty miles long, running southeast from the Bay of Acco at modern Haifa.

I traveled the full length of this historic range with Dr. Zev Vilnay, author of *The Guide to Israel* and a famed Israeli historian. Crowning one of the highest peaks, we came across the Monastery of Elijah. Beside it towered a statue of Elijah challenging the prophets of Baal. His challenge was appropriate, for Baal was the god of the storm, the god controlling the weather. On the mount, the impotence of the false prophets of Baal was unmasked.

From the heights of Carmel, as we looked down into the Valley of Esdraelon with the Kidron River flowing through it, we recalled how the 400 prophets of Baal and the 450 prophets of Asherah were slain beside this very stream.

The Carmel range juts out to the Bay of Acco at Haifa on the Mediterranean Sea. On its summit stands the Carmelite Monastery, the world headquarters of the Carmelite Order of the Roman Catholic Church. The lavishly ornamented altar of Elijah within is almost without a rival in its magnificence.

Considerably less ostentatious is the small white chapel on the side of the hill below the monastery, said to be built over the cave in which Elijah dwelt. The pious believe that when Elijah returns to earth, it will be to this abode. So pilgrims come here for the healing of their maladies and also to await his coming.

The coming of the Assyrians

Shalmaneser III was king of Assyria during the period when Ahab ruled in Israel. His capital was at Nimrud, the biblical Calah, twenty-four miles south of Mosul in modern Iraq. He was the first Assyrian king to make contact with the northern tribes of Israel.

My first visit to Mosul and the surrounding territory from which the Assyrians once vaunted their power was by Nairn bus from Damascus to Baghdad, then by train to Mosul. The Nairn bus, built on a semitruck chassis, is manufactured in the United States for this special desert run. Built to accommodate forty-five people, it took us directly across the weary desert sands. Since there were forty-six in our group, I volunteered to ride in a second bus with Arab passengers.

My friends left first. In the distance I saw a trail of dust as their bus left the pavement.

My bus housed not only the passengers, including a group returning from a sacred pilgrimage to Mecca, but most everything they possessed—bags of personal belongings, boxes of everything imaginable, including crates of chickens. There was also a goat or two—just about everything, including plenty of sick and crying children. The travel route was strictly by the way of the camels—directly across the lonely, wearisome desert sands.

I was miserable. The bus was supposedly air conditioned, but there was little evidence of it. With the windows closed, it was unbearably hot. With the windows open, the dust from the wheels came surging through.

The distance was about six hundred miles. Fortunately, about half way, we reached a paved road coming north from Amman, Jordan. It was an unforgettable journey of twenty-four hours. The long, snakelike trailer-bus left Damascus at noon and arrived in Baghdad at noon the next day.

From Baghdad we took the all-night train to Mosul, 220 miles north. Arriving in the early morning, taxis took us south to Nimrud. Here, before the ancient mound fronting the temple tower, we saw the site of the palace of Shalmaneser III, which had been excavated by Austin Henry Layard in 1845—among the earliest of the Assyrian palaces to be excavated.

Finds from an Assyrian palace

Shalmaneser (859-824 B.C.) campaigned during thirty-five years of his reign and left fascinating reliefs of his conquests on his palace walls. In the throne room, which seemed to serve as the administrative center, one hundred inscribed clay tablets were found.

One of the tablets described the Battle of Qarqar that was fought along the Orontes River in north Syria. In it, Shalmaneser was opposed by a coalition of ten kings, including "Ahab the Israelite." The nation of Israel must have been the strongest of the ten, for Ahab had supplied 2,000 of the 3,940 chariots used, and 10,000 of the 52,000 foot soldiers. Since this battle is not mentioned in Scripture, we have in this inscription a good example of how archaeology supplements the Bible.

The Assyrian king's palace also produced an abundance of ivory artifacts, ornaments that must have been as popular with him as they were with Ahab.

The excavations produced one of Assyria's most famous monuments—the Black Obelisk of Shalmaneser III. Standing six and a half feet high, the black limestone pillar is surrounded with five rows of bas reliefs. Of particular interest is the second panel from the top. It shows a figure kneeling before the king, to whom tribute is borne. The inscription below the panel reads, "Tribute of Jehu, son of Omri. I received from him silver, gold, a golden bowl, a golden vase with pointed bottom, golden tumblers, tin, a staff for a king . . ."

It was Jehu who brought the Omri-Ahab dynasty to an end in 841 B.C. In this inscription we have both his name and his picture. Shalmaneser also refers to Hazael, king of Damascus. And in Scripture Elijah was bidden to anoint Hazael king over Syria (see 1 Kings 19:15). Again we observe how the Bible and archaeology complement each other.

While Israel under King Ahab fell into heathen worship, the kingdom of Judah to the south was doing much better. In Jerusalem, the good king Asa reigned for forty-one years. He was the first of the reformers of Judah. Of him, we read:

He took away the altars of the strange gods, and the high places, and brake down the images, and cut down the groves. . . . Also he took away out of all the cities of Judah the high places and the images: and the kingdom was quiet before him (2 Chronicles 14:3, 5).

His son, Jehoshaphat, who succeeded him to the throne, continued the work of reform. However, late in his fruitful twenty-five-year reign, he mistakenly permitted his son, Jehoram, to marry the daughter of Ahab and Jezebel. Their marriage led to the worship of Baal. Fortunately, Judah experienced reformations under good kings like Hezekiah and Josiah, and the nation lived on for another century and a half.

With Israel, it was different. None of her kings served the Lord. The brief revival under Elijah was the only one she ever knew. Her ears were closed to the voices calling for reform. So her days were numbered. Soon Israel would be taken captive into Assyria.

---

* John C. H. Laughlin, "The Remarkable Discoveries at Tel Dan," *BAR*, September/October 1981, 20-37; *BAR* Interview. "Avraham Biran—Twenty Years of Digging at Tel Dan," *BAR*, July/August 1987, 12ff.

Chapter 16

The Hittites— Fact or Fiction?

Among the principal nations encountered by the Israelites were the Hittites. They are mentioned forty-eight times in the Old Testament and were a dominant power in the world throughout most of the Old Testament period.

Abraham purchased a cave from the Hittites in which to bury his wife. Esau married a Hittite. The Hittites were among the seven nations in Palestine at the time of Israel's conquest of Canaan (see Genesis 26:34; 36:2; Numbers 13:29). The king of Jerusalem who wrote to Akhenaten, the Sun King, had a Hittite name. David had Hittite soldiers in his army. Solomon had Hittites in his forced labor camps and had lively trade dealings with them.

The Bible is full of references to the Hittites. But, strange as it may seem, until modern times their name was unknown outside the Bible. So the critics said the Bible is wrong—such a people never lived, or at least were unimportant.

Then came the amazing discoveries of archaeology. The finding of the lost Hittite Empire is one of the most fascinating sagas of exploration in the history of archaeology.[1]

In the summer of 1975, my wife and I, with another couple, Dr. and Mrs. Walter Brown, traveled five thousand miles through Turkey and north Syria. We rented a Renault 12 in Istanbul and traced the footsteps of the archaeologists in their rediscovery of the lost Hittite Empire.

My interest in this fascinating people had been aroused by the account Ramses the Great gave of his battle against the Hatti (Hittite) people at Kadesh on the Orontes River in northern Syria. I had seen his account inscribed on the walls of the Amon temple at Karnak. Until modern times, no one knew who the Hatti people were. So with great anticipation, we set out from Istanbul with cameras, plenty of film, and an array of guide books and maps.

The amazing story of the discovery of the Hittite civilization had its beginning in 1809 when an inscribed stone was found in a bazaar at Hamath in northern Syria. Although written with hieroglyphic characters similar to those used in Egypt, the inscription was not in Egyptian, but in a language never seen before.

In 1870, three similar stones were found in the Hamath bazaar. Others also came to light in Smyrna, the modern Ismir, on the Mediterranean coast.

In 1879 the prominent biblical scholar, Archibald Henry Sayce, examined the stones at Smyrna. He subsequently announced to the Society for Biblical Archaeology in London that the writing was that of the Hittites. Scholars laughed and called him the inventor of the Hittites.

Then similar inscriptions and other artifacts were found at Carchemish near the Syrian border, and at Boghazköy, 120 miles east of Ankara. So, at several places far removed from each other, evidence was found pointing to a people who must have inhabited this entire region of Asia Minor. Sayce insisted that they were the Hittites, but the scholars still laughed.

There was the unsolved mystery of the "Hatti" people with whom Rameses the Great had fought the Battle of Kadesh. Who were they? Sayce said they were the Hittites.

Whoever the Hatti were, they were a powerful enough nation to be reckoned with by even the great Thutmose III. In Mesopotamia, they attacked and captured Babylon in 1595 B.C., thus ending the old Babylonian dynasty that had flourished in the days of Hammurabi (1728-1676 B.C.).

A key find came in 1887 with the discovery of the tablets at Tel el-Amarna. The Amarna tablets clearly identified the Hatti people as the Hittites. The evidence was in. Sayce was right. The tablets spoke of numerous raids by the Hittites into Egypt and Syria and of extensive relations between the Hittites and Egypt. No longer could their existence as a substantial nation be questioned.

The Amarna tablets also gave evidence that the Hittite nation inhabited central Asia Minor. At Zinjirli in the southern foothills of the Taurus mountains, we visited the site where the first major excavation of Hittite remains was undertaken in 1888. And in the museum in Istanbul, we observed many of the huge objects that were among the eighty-two crates of Hittite remains found at Zinjirli.

Boghazköy—capital city

Of special interest were the excavations that began in 1906 at Boghazköy, 120 miles east of Ankara, the present capital of Turkey. We viewed the place where ten thousand inscribed tablets were found, the greatest find since the discoveries of the tablets at Tel el-Amarna and of the famed library of King Ashurbanipal at Nineveh.

Many of the tablets from Boghazköy were government documents, a striking evidence that this had been the Hittites' capital city. Further excavations revealed that the capital had existed for about 350 years, from 1650 to 1200 B.C., when it fell to the Sea Peoples.

Among the startling finds at Boghazköy were the Hittite account of the famous Battle of Kadesh and the treaty subsequently entered into, the first international treaty of which we have a detailed account.

In Rameses' version of the battle, the king is portrayed as a great hero. According to the Hittite report, if shock troops had not come to his rescue in the nick of time, Rameses would have been captured.

Our visit to Boghazköy took us through the ancient gateway

into the citadel that is guarded by massive stone lions. We walked along the royal road beside courtyards and palaces. Then we drove up the mountain ridge that surrounds the city. We passed several temple sites and drove on to the massive stone wall on top of the ridge—a miniature of the Great Wall of China. We stood amazed before the towering stone gateways that pierced the wall at different intervals. The King's Gate, the Sphinx Gate, and the Lion Gate are all guarded by enormous stone creatures that towered over our heads. At one point we walked through a 220-foot tunnel carved beneath the immense wall.

Returning to the citadel, we drove another couple of miles or so to the great open-air rock sanctuary of Yazilkaya. This rock shrine, fronted by a vast temple complex, was the Hittites' most significant national religious center. Within the rock citadel we viewed the parade of Hittite gods carved in the rock wall.

Then we took the winding road to Alacahoyuk, several miles' distance, where we passed through another colossal sphinx gateway and walked down sacred Procession Street. On either side, we saw the remains of ancient temple and palace buildings uncovered by the archaeologists. We would later see a partial restoration of the sphinx gateway in the Hittite Museum in Ankara.

After the fall of Boghazköy, the great Hittite Empire was divided into small city-states, the most important of which was Carchemish. When Carchemish fell to the Assyrians in 717 B.C., the impressive Hittite civilization came to an end and was forgotten until modern times.

At Carchemish we saw excavations, dug by archaeologists between 1911 and 1914, that produced amazing results. A featured attraction in the Ankara Hittite Museum are the lengthy rows of inscribed reliefs that once adorned the walls of the city—scenes of battle and of victory over their enemies.

The riddle of the Hittite hieroglyphic

The excavations at Boghazköy, Carchemish, and other

sites revealed three different languages—Akkadian, Hittite, and an unknown language in hieroglyphic.

Akkadian was a common language during the Hittite time. It had already been deciphered before the excavations began. The Hittite cuneiform language was deciphered in 1917.

The strange hieroglyphic writings were identical to those that had appeared first on the stones in a bazaar at Hamath in northern Syria and later on stones found in Smyrna, both more than one hundred years before. But they were not deciphered until after 1947, when a lengthy bilingual inscription was found high atop the black mountain of Karatepe. And herein lies another fascinating story.

In a little village near Kadrili, Helmuth Bossert got word of a stone lion on the top of the black mountain (Karatepe). This was surely a Hittite ruin awaiting exploration. At that time the Karatepe mountain was almost inaccessible. Bossert made his first ascent as far as possible by horse-drawn wagon, then continued on horseback until forced to walk the final distance through the dense underbrush.

He found the stone lion and other evidence of major Hittite remains. Two subsequent trips up the mountain and considerable work disclosed an ancient palace. But most important was the discovery on his third ascent, March 15, 1947, of a lengthy bilingual inscription that proved to be the key to the decipherment of the strange Hittite hieroglyphic writing.

We wondered if the site on top of the mountain would be accessible to us. Fortunately, a recently constructed paved highway going north from Tarsus, home of the apostle Paul, took us to Kadrili at the foot of the mountain. Then, while driving through the village, we were delighted to find a sign pointing up the hill to Karatepe.

About fifteen miles of steady climbing along a narrow, winding road took us to the summit. To our surprise, the ancient Hittite citadel has been converted into a large open-air museum. Excavations have exposed the characteristic stone lions and other creatures and the ancient palace walls that are paneled with reliefs similar to those at Carchemish.

When Bossert visited the site in 1947, all hope of ever deciphering the strange hieroglyphic writing had been given up, because the chance of finding a bilingual inscription was remote. However, here the great discovery was made. One of the languages was the well-known Phoenician, the longest Phoenician inscription yet discovered. The second language was the evasive Hittite written with the hieroglyphic characters. With this bilingual script it would be possible to crack the mystery of the language that had baffled experts for over a hundred years.

The Hittite Waterloo

The amazing Hittites finally were destroyed by the cruel war machine of the Assyrians. In 743 B.C., Tiglath-pileser III defeated the Hittite king of Carchemish, the one remaining independent city-state. Then in 717 B.C., Sargon II returned to Carchemish, captured the Hittite king, and took the capital city. Inscriptions from Carchemish show that Sargon then rebuilt the city as the headquarters of an Assyrian province.

The Bible vindicated

The amazing discovery of the lost Hittite Empire stands out as a remarkable testimony to the reliability of the Bible. Doubting scholars had for more than a century challenged the existence of such a people, despite the numerous references to them in the Bible, or had at least insisted that they had never been a people of any consequence.

Thanks to the spade of the archaeologists, the entire picture has changed. The Hittites stand forth boldly today as one of the major powers of the ancient world. The Bible has scored again. Its claims have again been vindicated. Its pages produce facts, not fiction.

---

1. See C. W. Ceram, *The Secret of the Hittites* (New York: Alfred A. Knopf, 1956).

Chapter 17

The Assyrian War Machine

The same ruthless war machine that spelled disaster to the Hittites was used by God to bring judgment upon the northern kingdom of Israel. The Assyrians, who are mentioned 130 times in the Old Testament, had a long history. They were the first great empire to come into existence after the Flood. Nimrod, the grandson of Noah, "went forth into Assyria, and builded Nineveh, and the city Rehoboth-Ir, and Calah" (Genesis 10:11, ASV).

The Assyrians occupied the northern part of Mesopotamia that came to be known as Akkad. Sometimes Assyria was weak, sometimes strong. Sometimes it exerted its independence. At other times it was forced to pay tribute to neighboring kingdoms.

In the days of Abraham, Assyria was a part of the kingdom of Ur. After the eclipse of the third dynasty of Ur, about 1900 B.C., Assyria became an independent sovereign state. Then, with the rise of the powerful Hammurabi in the eighteenth century B.C., it became subject to the Babylonian kingdom for about 150 years. After that, its power oscillated back and forth—sometimes strong, sometimes weak—often subject to Babylon.

Gradually it managed to exert its independence, and by the middle of the fourteenth century B.C., Assyria had become a significant power. In 1274 B.C. Shalmaneser I came to the throne, expanded the kingdom, and established his capital at the biblical Calah, the present Nimrud.

After the reign of Shalmaneser I, there were again periods of decline and clashes between Assyria and Babylon. But when the powerful Tiglath-pileser I (1115-1077 B.C.) came to the throne, he led the Assyrians to a new period of greatness by marching his armies all the way to Phoenicia on the Mediterranean.

By the time of his death, however, Assyrian power was again waning, and there followed a succession of weak kings, and for 150 years she had her Dark Age. Things improved under Ashurdan, who was followed in 885 B.C. by the powerful and aggressive Ashurnasirpal II (885-859 B.C.). After his reign, Assyria remained the most powerful nation on earth for almost three hundred years.

Nimrud, archaeology, and the kings

Ashurnasirpal's magnificent palace at Nimrud was among the first of the Assyrian palaces to be unearthed.

In 1839, twenty-two-year-old Austin Henry Layard of London wandered adventurously through the deserts of Asia Minor and Syria, riding on horseback with his wardrobe behind his saddle. He rode without regard to comfort or danger, accompanied by one companion who would later, out of fear, forsake him.

Without guides or servants, twice robbed, and often at great risk, the two pressed on from tribe to tribe. Then one day they rode into Mosul. Soon they were looking over the mound of Nimrud, twenty-four miles to the south. Layard was convinced that beneath this mound lay the ancient city of Nineveh. He determined that someday he would return to excavate.

Six years later, on November 8, 1845, the dauntless Layard, now alone, sailed down the Tigris River toward the realization of his dream. During the six years of his absence, the entire region had become alive with insurrection; but, winning the confidence of the tribal sheik, he hired six Arab workmen, all he could afford, and began the excavations.

He met success from the very first.[1] Soon huge slabs from the palace, later identified as that of Ashurnasirpal, appeared. The walls were covered with beautifully carved reliefs, most of which were removed and may be seen in the British Museum. Thirteen pairs of winged lions and bulls were also taken from the ground. The recovery of a single bull required a trench ninety feet long, twelve feet wide, and twenty-two feet deep.

Many tablets were found that describe the exploits of Ashurnasirpal, and today this king is a familiar figure. When he assumed the throne in 885 B.C., he set out at once to extend the power of the nation. Many of the scenes of his exploits are graphically depicted, including many that depict the system of cruelty he introduced, all calculated to strike terror in his enemies. He boasted:

In the midst of the mighty mountain I slaughtered them, with their blood I dyed the mountain red like wool. . . . The heads of their warriors I cut off, and I formed them into a pillar over against their city, their young men and their maidens I burned in the fire.[2]

Again he declared,

I built a pillar over against the city gate, and I flayed all the chief men who had revolted, and I covered the pillar with their skins. . . . I cut off the limbs of the officers, of the royal officers who rebelled.[3]

The lesson was clear—you had better be good!

The dedication of the king's palace is described at length on a stele found by Mallowan in the 1950s. It was a most impressive celebration. There were 69,572 guests, including 5,000 foreign emissaries and 1,500 officials from other Assyrian palaces. The feast lasted ten days, and 2,200 oxen, 16,000 sheep, 10,000 skins of wine, and 10,000 barrels of beer were consumed.

Having visited Nimrud in 1957, I was surprised on my return visit in 1988 at the extent of the restoration accomplished during the intervening years. Considerable portions of the palace of Ashurnasirpal had been restored. I walked through the huge gateways, fronted by the Assyrian winged bulls, and into the courtyards, halls, and chambers of the ancient king. Some of the walls still hold slabs of sculptured alabaster, including portraits of the monarch.

In April 1989, a team of Iraqi archaeologists, while digging within the palace, came across a major find—a tomb containing a sarcophagus with the remains of two women and 125 pounds of golden crafted articles. According to Dr. David Stronach, professor of Near Eastern archaeology at the University of California, Berkeley, "This is the single richest royal tomb ever excavated" in that part of the world. "It is possible that one of the women was a queen or daughter of Sargon II." Sargon (722-705 B.C.) was the conqueror of Samaria. The treasure included fifty pairs of gold earrings.[4]

In July 1989, a second tomb was opened that contained fifty pounds of gold. Early suggestions are that this second tomb was that of the queen of Ashurnasirpal. The jewelry displays an amazing craftsmanship, far superior to what might be expected.

The discovery of these tombs, found under the private quarters of the palace, has been acclaimed the most significant find since the opening of the tomb of King Tutankhamen in 1922.

Shalmaneser III

Ashurnasirpal was succeeded to the throne by his son, Shalmaneser III (859-824 B.C.), who added still more territory to the great empire. He described himself as "the sun of all peoples, despot of all lands." Almost all of his thirty-five-year reign was spent on the battlefield.

The Assyrians were the scourge of the known world. The Bible speaks of them as coming like a "whirlwind," "roaring . . .

like a lion," leaving darkness and sorrow (Isaiah 5:28, 29).

We marvel at the appropriateness of the words of the prophet Nahum directed against Assyria:

> The noise of a whip, and the noise of the rattling of the wheels, and of the prancing horses, and of the jumping chariots. The horseman lifteth up both the bright sword and the glittering spear: and there is a multitude of slain, and a great number of carcases; and there is none end of their corpses; they stumble upon their corpses (Nahum 3:2, 3).

The Assyrian texts relate how Shalmaneser III, the first Assyrian king to come into contact with Israel, fought against Ahab in the Battle of Qarqar on the Orontes in 853 B.C. The texts also tell how, twelve years later, he received tribute from Jehu, king of Israel. In this way the biblical records are expanded and illuminated.

Shalmaneser was followed by several weak kings, and during the next eighty years much of the territory he had gained was lost. It was probably during this time that Jonah made his remarkable appearance in Nineveh, the Assyrian capital. Considering the fierceness and savagery of the Assyrians, we can readily understand Jonah's reluctance to go to Nineveh.

During this same period of Assyria's decline, Israel's king, Jeroboam II, took advantage of her weakness and restored much of the territory to Israel that had been lost since the time of Solomon.

Tiglath-pileser III and the Bible

This period of Assyria's decline gave way to a great resurgence under Tiglath-pileser III (745-727 B.C.), who became one of Assyria's greatest monarchs and empire builders. Continuing to govern from Nimrud, he built a lavish palace and decorated its walls with the story of his conquests.

Babylon had been taken, then lost, by Assyria a number of times. Now, under the name "Pul," Tiglath-pileser proclaimed himself "king of Babylon."

Among his military campaigns were those against Syria and Palestine. In the Bible we read,

Pul the king of Assyria came against the land: and Menahem [the king of Israel] gave Pul a thousand talents of silver, that his hand might be with him to confirm the kingdom in his hand (2 Kings 15:19).

On an inscription of Tiglath-pileser we read,

As for Menahem, terror overwhelmed him, like a bird, alone he fled and submitted to me. To his place I brought him back and . . . silver, colored woolen garments, linen garments . . . I received as his tribute.[5]

The biblical record of the kings states how a few years later Tiglath-pileser returned: "In the days of Pekah king of Israel came Tiglath-Pileser king of Assyria . . . and carried them captive to Assyria" (2 Kings 15:29).

Tiglath-pileser also refers to this, saying, "Israel (lit.: 'Omri-Land', *Bît Humria*) . . . all its inhabitants (and) their possessions I led to Assyria."[6]

Pekah was slain in a conspiracy, and Hoshea became ruler of Israel (see 2 Kings 15:30). Of this Tiglath-pileser boasted:

"They overthrew their king Pekah [*Pa-qa-ha*] and I placed Hoshea [*A-ú-si-'*] as king over them. I received from them 10 talents of gold, 1,000 [?] talents of silver as their [tri]bute and brought them to Assyria."[7]

The biblical text states that "the king of Assyria went up against Damascus" (2 Kings 16:9).

Tiglath-pileser records:

"I received tribute from Kushtashpi of Commagene [*Kummuhu*], Rezon [*Ra-hi-a-nu*] of Damascus [*Sa-imërisu*], Menahem of Samaria [*Me-ni-hi-im-me Sa-me-ri-na-a-a*].[8]

The Assyrian inscription also states that Ahaz, king of Judah, became Tiglath-pileser's vassal and paid him tribute. There are also texts that speak of Tiglath-pileser's conquests of Babylonia and Media, events not mentioned in the Scriptures.

The fascinating reliefs in Tiglath-pileser's palace present interesting sidelights that reveal how archaeology sheds light on the customs portrayed in the Bible. The reliefs depict three men, in each chariot. The Bible mentions the "lord [or servant] on whose hand the king leaned" (2 Kings 7:2). This is a reference to the third person, or servant, who was the "strap hanger." He protected the king from falling back as the chariot lurched forward.

Tiglath-pileser III was succeeded by his son Shalmaneser V (727-722 B.C.). When Israel stopped paying tribute, Shalmaneser laid siege to their capital city of Samaria. The siege, which began about 724 B.C., continued for three long years. Shalmaneser died during the siege, but it was continued by Sargon II, who took the city of Samaria and led Israel into captivity. Three years later, Sargon brought about the demise of the Hittite Empire with the capture of Carchemish and her king.

The captivity of Israel

God used the ruthless Assyrians to chastise and punish His people Israel because of their refusal to heed the voice of the prophets calling them to repentance. The Bible records His awesome acts:

Yet the Lord testified against Israel, and against Judah, by all the prophets, and by all the seers, saying, Turn ye from your evil ways, and keep my commandments and my statutes, according to all the law which I commanded your fathers, and which I sent to you by my servants the prophets. Notwithstanding they would not hear, but hardened their necks. . . . And they rejected his statutes, and his covenant that he made with their fathers, and his testimonies which he testified against them. . . . And they left all the commandments of the Lord their God, and made them molten images, even two calves, and made a grove, and worshipped all the host of heaven, and served Baal. . . . Therefore the Lord was very angry with Israel, and removed them out of his sight: there was none left but the tribe of Judah only. . . . So was Israel carried away out of their own land to Assyria unto this day (2 Kings 17:13-16, 18, 23).

The ten tribes were dispersed into remote regions of Assyria. Only a remnant of the poorest of the land remained in Israel. They intermarried with the imported Assyrians and became the Samaritans, who are often mentioned in the Scriptures. A small remnant of Samaritans survive today. They live in the village of Nablus at the site of ancient Shechem. Their priests display their sacred scrolls, which they claim are the only true version of the Old Testament Scriptures.

Sargon at Samaria and Ashdod

After assuming the throne, Sargon erected a lavish palace at Khorsabad, fifteen miles north of Mosul. He erected the first Assyrian palace discovered by archaeologists when they began excavating in Mesopotamia in 1840. As we walked over the site, we saw stones from the ancient palace scattered on the grounds.

The king's palace, fronted by colossal winged bulls with human heads, had massive walls covered with decorative reliefs. When the name Sargon first appeared, the scholars blushed. Up to that time the name Sargon was unknown except in the Bible, and the critics had questioned whether such a person had ever lived. Isaiah 20:1 says, "In the year that Tartan came unto Ashdod (when Sargon the king of Assyria sent him,) and fought against Ashdod and took it."

The discovery of Sargon's palace is the first example of the archaeologist's work bringing to light an inscription that authenticates a specific Bible reference.

In 1846 a large collection of Assyrian antiquities was taken to the Louvre museum in Paris, the first collection of such artifacts in Europe. In the Louvre we saw the colossal bulls that once fronted the gateway of Sargon's palace, and we viewed in wonderment the lengthy reliefs from the palace walls. In Baghdad, we entered the archaeological museum by way of a restored gateway from Sargon's palace.

The Oriental Institute at the University of Chicago excavated at Khorsabad from 1919 to 1935. On display at the institute is another of the colossal bulls from Sargon's palace and many of the walled reliefs. Of particular interest are the reliefs showing captives being taken to Assyria. Among them were the Israelites.

In one inscription, Sargon says:

"I besieged and captured Samaria, carrying off 27,290 of the people who dwelt therein. 50 chariots I gathered from among them, I caused others to take their [the deported inhabitants'] portion, I set my officers over them and imposed upon them the tribute of the former king."[9]

Sargon styled himself as the "lord of the four quarters of the earth." Fourteen barrel cylinders that contain historical records were found in his palace. They include many of the names and places we read of in the Bible.

One of them refers to Sargon's campaign against Ashdod, the very campaign mentioned in Isaiah. It reads:

In a sudden rage, I did not (wait to) assemble the full

might of my army (or to) prepare the camp(ing equipment), but started out towards Ashdod (only) with those
of my warriors who, even in friendly areas, never leave
my side. . . . I besieged (and) conquered the cities Ashdod,
Gath, Asdudimmu.[10]

At the Philistine city of Ashdod, archaeologists, working
there since 1962, uncovered striking evidence of the destruction caused by Sargon. These included skeletons and bones
belonging to some three thousand persons who probably
perished during the conquest of the city. Also found were
three fragments of a basalt stele set up to memorialize the
victory. Another just like it had previously been found at
Khorsabad.

Looking again at Isaiah 20:1, we note the words, "In the
year that Tartan came unto Ashdod." Translators of the King
James Version concluded Tartan to be a proper name. Now
the Assyrian inscriptions reveal that Tartan is a title, meaning "Commander in Chief."

So modern translations reflect the historical evidence uncovered by the archaeologist. As an example, in   Today's
English Version, Isaiah 20:1 reads:

> Under the orders of Emperor Sargon of Assyria, the
> *commander-in-chief* of the Assyrian army attacked the
> Philistine city of Ashdod (italics supplied).

A prize find at Khorsabad was a tablet now known as the
Khorsabad King List. Beginning with the thirty-third Assyrian
king, it lists the names of the successive kings and the years
of their reign and is, thus, a great aid in establishing a correct
chronology of the Assyrian kings.

A similar king list was found in a most unexpected manner in
1953 by Dr. Siegfried Horn. While visiting in the home of a
missionary family in Baghdad, he noticed the children playing
with an old clay tablet. Out of curiosity he picked it up, and to

his great surprise he recognized that it was a list of Assyrian kings similar to the Khorsabad King List.

Up to that time the Khorsabad King List had not been published and made available to scholars, much to their distress. Now the two lists were published simultaneously.[11] The latter, known as the SDAS (Seventh-day Adventist Seminary) Assyrian King List, is now on display along with the Khorsabad King List in the Iraqi Archaeological Museum in Baghdad.

The reliefs and other artifacts of Sargon have greatly illuminated this important period of Israel's history. We can now read the Scriptures with renewed confidence and in the context of the secular history of the surrounding nations.

1. For an interesting account, read Arnold C. Brackman, *The Luck of Nineveh* (New York: McGraw-Hill, 1978).

2. Finegan, *Light From the Ancient East*, 170.

3. Ibid., 170, 171.

4. *Los Angeles Times*, 13 November 1989.

5. Finegan, *Light From the Ancient Past*, 173.

6. Pritchard, *The Ancient Near East*, 194.

7. Ibid.

8. Ibid., 193.

9. Finegan, *Light From the Ancient Past*, 175.

10. Pritchard, *The Ancient Near East*, 197.

11. *Journal of Near Eastern Studies* (October 1954).

Chapter 18

Hezekiah
and Sennacherib

For over three centuries, Jerusalem served as the capital of Israel. At first, Jerusalem was capital of the united kingdom of all twelve tribes of Israel. Then, when the ten northern tribes seceded in 931 B.C. and established a capital at Shechem, Jerusalem became the capital of Judah, as the southern kingdom was called.

King Ahaz was on the throne in Jerusalem when the Assyrians carried the first of the northern tribes into captivity in 722 B.C. He was succeeded by his son Hezekiah, who was determined to save Judah from the fate of the northern kingdom.

Hezekiah's call for revival

Great reforms were instituted. It was a time of revival. Ahaz had closed the doors of the sanctuary and discontinued its services. Altars for the worship of heathen gods had been set up on street corners throughout the city. Heathenism seemed to triumph.

But now, under Hezekiah's leadership, the heathen altars were torn down, the temple cleansed and repaired, and the doors thrown open. Again the people gathered from far and wide for the celebration of the Passover Feast.

Hezekiah's tunnel

King Hezekiah ranks as one of the great builders in Old

Testament times. With the cruel Assyrians pillaging the cities of the northern tribes and taking captives, he knew it wouldn't be long until they would be at the gates of Jerusalem.

Anticipating this, he rebuilt the old defensive walls and added an outer wall. Excavations on the eastern slopes of the mount of Ophel have uncovered parts of his work.

One of Hezekiah's principal achievements was digging a tunnel that would provide water in case of a siege. Second Kings 20:20 states that Hezekiah "made a pool, and a conduit, and brought water into the city."

To accomplish this, the king covered the top of the spring of Gihon that was located outside the walls of Jerusalem. He then dug a tunnel 1,750 feet long to the Pool of Siloam, which was within the walls. A walk through this ancient tunnel in knee-deep running water is an unforgettable experience.

In 1880, a lad was playing a few yards inside the tunnel when he noticed some scratchings on the wall. These scratchings turned out to be Hezekiah's own account of his digging project.

The inscription, today a prized possession of the Museum of the Ancient Orient at Istanbul, reads:

"The boring through [is completed]. And this is the story of the boring through: while yet [they plied] the drill, each toward his fellow, and while yet there were three cubits to be bored through, there was heard the voice of one calling unto another, for there was crevice in the rock on the right hand. And on the day of the boring through the stone-cutters struck, each to meet his fellow, drill upon drill; and the water flowed from the source to the pool for a thousand and two hundred cubits, and a hundred cubits was the height of the rock above the heads of the stone-cutters."[1]

While Hezekiah was strengthening his position in Jerusalem, the Assyrians besieged and captured Samaria and scattered Israel's ten tribes among Assyria's many provinces. After leading the final assault on Israel in 722 B.C., Sargon II continued to extend the might of his empire. At his death seventeen years later, the powerful kingdom was inherited by his son Sennacherib (705-681 B.C.).

The wonders of Sennacherib

Sennacherib moved Assyria's capital to Nineveh, along the left bank of the Tigris, just outside of present-day Mosul. Under his rule, the city became the wealthiest and most resplendent capital of the then-known world, surpassing by far the capital city his father Sargon had built at Khorsabad. Massive walls stretched for two and a half miles along the Tigris and eight miles around the city. The walls were pierced by fifteen mighty gateways. Great lengths of the wall and several of the gateways have been restored in recent years.

Layard's excavations of Sennacherib's palace turned out to be his most glorious achievement. It had stood as "The Palace Without a Rival." It was so embellished with gold that "the whole city shone like the sun."

In his excavations Layard opened up no less than seventy-one halls, chambers, and passages. In his journal he wrote:

By a rough calculation, about 9,880 feet, nearly two miles of bas-reliefs, with twenty-seven portals formed by colossal winged bull and lion-sphinxes, were uncovered in that part alone of the building explored during my researches.[2]

Today many of these reliefs make up one of the principal exhibits in the world-famous British Museum.

Sennacherib, a cruel monarch, continued the fiendish policies inaugurated by Ashurnasirpal about 180 years before. In 689 B.C., he decided to erase Babylon from the face of the earth. Reliefs in the British Museum portray the battle. Horse-drawn chariots are prominent, and earth ramparts and siege ramps are clearly depicted. The reliefs portray in striking detail the armed soldiers hastening on to battle. Eagerly, armed with arrows, their faces stern and fixed, they move toward their prey. The bowmen are shown scaling the walls. Some carry slings for hurling stones and fire. Then captives are shown being escorted by their victors.

In other scenes, captives are shown bringing tribute to their Assyrian conquerors, while others prostrate themselves on the ground with pleas for mercy. We marvel at the Assyrian artistry that was etched in stone almost 2,700 years ago.

Evidence of Sennacherib's work may also be seen in the far north of Iraq at Jerwan, northeast of Mosul. Here the waters of natural springs are directed into a huge aqueduct that is said to be the world's oldest. The cliffs near the springs and the huge blocks of stone of the aqueduct are decorated with carvings and cuneiform inscriptions by the king.

The Bible has much to say about Sennacherib. In 2 Kings 18:13 we read:

Now in the fourteenth year of king Hezekiah did Sennacherib king of Assyria come up against all the fenced cities of Judah, and took them.

The siege of Lachish

Sennacherib's war against Hezekiah was a major campaign about which he himself had much to report. According to his annals, some forty-six towns of Judah fell to him. The mightiest of these and the last to fall was Lachish. It was about twenty miles southwest of Jerusalem and guarded the approach from the lowlands.

This battle against Judah must have been the most important battle of Sennacherib's entire career, for scenes of the battle were used to grace the walls of the throne room of his palace. Now in the British Museum, they enable us to relive the frightful battle down to its minutest detail.

The reliefs depict the Assyrians, at the foot of the city walls, attacking with great violence and with a variety of weapons.

Each soldier is armed to the teeth and is protected by his shield and helmet. Siege engines, the first tanks in history, are shown pushing forward up ramps built of earth. In front of the siege engines, battering rams stick out like the barrel of a cannon. Archers are seen behind a protective canopy. In addition to conventional arrows, they hurl stones and burning torches—the firebombs of the ancient world.

The scenes show Sennacherib following the treacherous practices of the kings before him, flaying the captives and hanging them up on pointed stakes.

The surrender of the city is clearly depicted. A procession of prisoners is taken, along with the spoil. The Assyrians stand guard while the unwilling captives in humble submission, some in prostrate form, are received by the king on his throne. The king declares:

> Sennacherib, king of the world, king of Assyria, sat upon a *nîmedu*-throne and passed in review the booty (taken) from Lachish (*La-Ki-su*).[3]

Lachish, the scene of the frightful battle, was first excavated from 1932 to 1938. The dig was resumed in 1973 and is continuing as one of Israel's most fascinating archaeological projects.

The 1 May 1978 edition of the *Jerusalem Post* came out with the headline, "Sennacherib's Ramp Discovered." The news story indicated that the fighting seems to have centered at the principal gateway, the largest ever found in Palestine. In the three feet of debris encountered, actual slings and sling stones from the battle were found.

In November 1987, I saw archaeologists enthusiastically engaged in restoring the gateway. Once completed, Lachish will become a national park and a prominent tourist site.

Sennacherib attacks Jerusalem

Among the most significant finds relating to Sennacherib

was his famous hexagon prism, found in his palace at Nineveh, and now in the British Museum. Known as the Prism of Sennacherib, it describes the king's expeditions into Judah, including his campaign against Jerusalem that is familiar to Bible students. The inscription reads in part,

> As to Hezekiah, the Jew, he did not submit to my yoke, I laid siege to 46 of his strong cities. . . . I drove out (of them) 200,150 people. . . . Himself I made a prisoner in Jerusalem, his royal residence, like a bird in a cage. . . . I still increased the tribute and the *katrû*-presents (due) to me (as his) overlord which I imposed (later) upon him beyond the former tribute, to be delivered annually.[4]

Sennacherib goes on to record the amount of tribute Hezekiah was forced to send to him, which included "thirty talents of gold."

In 2 Kings 18:14 we read, "The king of Assyria appointed unto Hezekiah king of Judah three hundred talents of silver and thirty talents of gold."

A comparison of the two accounts is significant. It is clear from both sources that Sennacherib never did take Jerusalem, but settled for tribute. After the invasion of Sennacherib, King Hezekiah revolted against him. This led to a second campaign against Jerusalem thirteen years after the first (see 2 Kings 18, 19; 2 Chronicles 32; Isaiah 36, 37).

Now it is known from archaeological discoveries that at the time of the first campaign Tirhakah was only about nine years old, and that in 690 B.C. he began to reign as coregent in Egypt. Therefore the scriptural reference to him cannot go back as early as 701 B.C., the date of Sennacherib's first campaign. The presence of his name in this text therefore requires a second campaign. So the Bible is right again.

Of this second campaign, Isaiah declared:

> Thus saith the Lord concerning the king of Assyria, He

shall not come into this city, nor shoot an arrow there, nor come before it with shield, nor cast a bank against it. By the way that he came, by the same shall he return (2 Kings 19:32, 33).

The record then describes the disastrous defeat:

And it came to pass that night, that the angel of the Lord went out, and smote in the camp of the Assyrians an hundred fourscore and five thousand (2 Kings 19:35).

Now notice how death came to the king:

So Sennacherib king of Assyria departed, and went and returned, and dwelt at Nineveh. And it came to pass, as he was worshipping . . . his sons smote him with the sword. . . . And Esarhaddon his son reigned in his stead (2 Kings 19:36, 37).

Esarhaddon also reports on the death of his father, Sennacherib, and his own elevation to the throne:

A firm determination fell upon my brothers. They forsook the gods and turned to their deeds of violence, plotting evil. . . . To gain the kingship they slew Sennacherib their father.[5]

Isaiah provides the names Adrammelech and Sharezer as the brothers who slew their father.

And it came to pass, as he was worshipping in the house of Nisroch his god, that Adrammelech and Sharezer his sons smote him with the sword; and they escaped into the land of Armenia: and Esarhaddon his son reigned in his stead (Isaiah 37:38).

Critics were once quick to point out that, according to contemporary Assyrian legal documents, Sennacherib was slain by his son Arad-Ninlil. This theory later gave way to an interpretation, according to which Esarhaddon, the heir-designate and successor to the throne, was thought to be the murderer. The debate among scholars has raged on. Recent studies, however, have again demonstrated the veracity of the Scriptures.

In an article published in 1980, entitled "The Murderer of Sennacherib," Simo Parpola of the University of Chicago gives the evidence.

Parpola reports that a Neo-Babylonian letter published decades ago explicitly states that Arad-Ninlil was the murderer, and from other documents Arad-Ninlil is known to be the son of Sennacherib. This Neo-Babylonian letter, states Parpola, makes Arad-Ninlil "the likeliest candidate for the murderer of Sennacherib, and in fact makes it a matter of virtual certainty." Parpola then points out that this name, translated from secular inscriptions as Arad-Ninlil, is the same name as the name Adrammelech found in the Bible. The problem resulted because the name Arad-Ninlil "was completely misunderstood and mistranslated by the editor" of the Assyrian inscriptions.[6] So the Bible scores again.

Parpola recaps the events leading to the murder of Sennacherib. Briefly stated, Esarhaddon, although not the eldest son, had been promised the throne. Adrammelech, however, enjoyed considerable popularity. As the years passed, the opposition to Esarhaddon grew, while Adrammelech and his brothers gained in popularity.

Foreseeing trouble, Sennacherib sent Esarhaddon away, yet he did not revise the order of succession. During his absence the brothers sought to take over the kingship by force. A "treaty of rebellion" was drawn up, and Sennacherib was slain.

Hearing of this, Esarhaddon swiftly attacked his rebellious brothers and hastened to Nineveh, where he secured the crown.[7]

1. George A. Barton, *Archaeology and the Bible* (Philadelphia: American Sunday-School Union, 1937), 476.

2. Arnold C. Brackman, *The Luck of Nineveh* (New York: McGraw-Hill, 1978), 3, 267; Merrill Unger, *Archeology and the Old Testament* (Grand Rapids: Zondervan, 1954), 263.

3. Pritchard, *The Ancient Near East*, 201.

4. Ibid., 200.

5. Unger, *Archaeology and the Old Testament*, 270.

6. Simo Parpola, "The Murderer of Sennacherib," in *Death in Mesopotamia*, 26th Rencontre Assyriologique Internationale Mesopotamia, vol. 8, ed. Bendt Acster (Copenhagen: Akademisk Forlag, 1980).

7. Adrammalech escaped punishment by fleeing to the "land of Ararat."

Chapter 19

The Last Days
of Assyria and Judah

Esarhaddon (680-669 B.C.) became another of Assyria's important kings. One of his achievements was the restoration of the city of Babylon that his father had destroyed. A relief depicts the king with a basket on his head rebuilding the temple tower. The fact that both his wife and mother were from Babylon may have contributed to his interest in the city.

Like other Assyrian kings, Esarhaddon engaged in extensive military campaigns, extending his dominion all the way through Palestine and down to Egypt. Inscriptions and reliefs of his campaigns are found in such faraway places as the Nahr El Kelb, which means Dog River, a few miles north of Beirut.

In the diggings at Zinjirli in Turkey, near the Syrian border, a victory stele of Esarhaddon was found, in which he boasts of his victory over Tirhakah of Egypt. His was a singular achievement, since Sennacherib had once been turned back by Tirhakah.

After the victory, Esarhaddon proudly boasts, "I am powerful, I am all powerful, I am a hero, I am gigantic, I am colossal."

Then, the first time for an Assyrian ruler, he takes the title, "King of the kings of Egypt."[1]

Esarhaddon's successful campaign against Tirhakah was probably a fulfillment of Isaiah's prophecy: "The Egyptians will I give over into the hand of a cruel Lord; and a fierce king shall rule over them, saith the Lord, the Lord of hosts" (Isaiah 19:4).

Visitors to the site of ancient Egypt are reminded of its destruction by this Assyrian king. Before Esarhaddon came, Memphis had stood as a capital city for many long centuries. He reduced it to ruins. A Zinjirli inscription describes the fateful battle:

Memphis his [Tirhakah's] royal city, in half a day, with mines, tunnels, assaults, I besieged, I captured, I destroyed, I devastated, I burned with fire.[2]

Esarhaddon left Nineveh for a second campaign against Egypt, but before reaching his destination, he died at Haran.

The fame of King Esarhaddon is being reborn. Described as "the greatest discovery of the century," archaeologists in the early summer of 1990 excavated the palace of Esarhaddon while digging in the mound of Nebi Younis, the mound of Jonah, at Nineveh. The removal of the seven colossal statues, half human and half animal, that stood guard over the entrance to the sumptuous palace is characterized by Manhal Jaber, director of the Iraqi excavators, as "the largest single haul in the history of Mesopotamian digs."

The massive mound of Nebi Younis, regarded as the site of the tomb of the prophet Jonah and crowned with a mosque, has previously been regarded as off limits to archaeologists. The discovery of Esarhaddon's palace, however, has led Iraq's antiquities department to declare the site as public cultural property. A mud village of about four hundred houses that had been erected on the artificial hill was removed.

One of the seven winged bulls was partially unearthed three years before while clearing ground with a bulldozer. The major dig is presently underway, exposing the palace gateway and walls that are decorated with marble slabs that depict mythological figures.

The restored palace of Esarhaddon is expected to turn Nebi Younis into a major tourist attraction.[3]

Ashurbanipal

After the death of Esarhaddon, his son, Ashurbanipal (669-633 B.C.) took the throne. He continued his father's second Egyptian campaign. After retaking Memphis, he moved south and captured Thebes, 450 miles up the Nile. In his graphic account of plundering the wealth of Thebes, he even puts forth the claim that he took two gigantic obelisks back to Assyria.

According to Homer, Thebes had one hundred gates. Until Ashurbanipal's invasion it had been considered impregnable. Excavations, however, confirm the great catastrophe that fell on the city at this time.

The cruel raid of Ashurbanipal is also described by the prophet Nahum, who wrote:

> Art thou better than populous No [Thebes], that was situate among the rivers, that had the waters round about it, whose rampart was the sea, and her wall was from the sea? . . . Yet was she carried away, she went into captivity: her young children also were dashed in pieces at the top of all the streets: and they cast lots for her honourable men, and all her great men were bound in chains (Nahum 3:8, 10).

Ashurbanipal became the last of the important Assyrian kings. The discovery of his vast palace and treasured library at Nineveh is one of the crowning achievements of archaeology. The reliefs from his palace walls are among the most magnificent of all Assyrian sculptures.

Although Ashurbanipal carried on extensive military campaigns, he is best known for his peaceful pursuits. He boasted of his skill as a hunter, and his lion-hunt sculptures are among the most impressive of all Assyrian reliefs.

The prophet Nahum mentions Nineveh as the dwelling place of lions:

Where is the dwelling of the lions, and the feedingplace of the young lions, where the lion, even the old lion, walked, and the lion's whelp, and none made them afraid? (Nahum 2:11).

Before the discovery of Nineveh's paneled reliefs, critics maintained that there were no lions in Mesopotamia, that the Bible was wrong. Now we know that lions were imported from Africa, then kept in captivity until released for the hunt—apparently the chief sport of the king. After being caught and killed, the lion would be taken to the temple and offered as a sacrifice to the gods.

Next to the lion room, Ashurbanipal's famous library was found. Its twenty thousand tablets have provided scholars with an amazing key to understanding the Assyrian-Babylonian civilization and have aided greatly in confirming the reliability of the Bible.

Nineveh in prophecy

Visitors to the ancient remains of the once proud city of Nineveh cannot help but recognize a remarkable fulfillment of Bible prophecy.

Zephaniah, who prophesied about 625 B.C., soon after the great and prosperous reign of Ashurbanipal had come to an end, declared:

He [the Lord] will . . . make Nineveh a desolation, and dry like a wilderness. And flocks shall lie down in the midst of her (Zephaniah 2:13, 14).

The prophet Nahum wrote concerning Nineveh:

I [the Lord of Hosts] will cast abominable filth upon thee, and make thee vile, and will set thee as a gazingstock. And it shall come to pass, that all they that look upon thee shall flee from thee, and say, Nineveh is laid waste (Nahum 3:6, 7).

So it is today. Nineveh fell to the Babylonian king Nabopolasser and the Medes in 612 B.C. So complete was her destruction that its very location was forgotten. When Xenophon and his ten thousand "immortals" passed by two hundred years later, no one could tell them the name of the city that had once stood where there were then only heaps of ruins. A few centuries later, the writer Lucian said that no one knew where Nineveh once stood.

What a remarkable fulfillment of Bible prophecy!

The destruction of Nineveh virtually brought to an end the cruel Assyrian Empire.

The prophet Nahum expresses well the feelings of the people who suffered the impact of the Assyrian tyranny:

> Thy shepherds slumber, O king of Assyria: thy nobles shall dwell in the dust: thy people is scattered upon the mountains, and no man gathereth them. There is no healing of thy bruise; thy wound is grievous: all that hear the bruit of thee shall clap the hands over thee: for upon whom hath not thy wickedness passed continually? (Nahum 3:18, 19).

The last days of Nineveh were graphically brought to light in startling excavations at the site in 1989/1990 by the University of California under the direction of Dr. David Stronach of the Berkeley campus. Diggings at one of the principal gates of the city, the Halzi Gate, uncovered amazing evidence of the final conflagration. This included the bodies of soldiers who perished in the onslaught, apparently crushed under a wall that had fallen.

The last days of Judah

When Assyria and its capital city, Nineveh, fell, Babylon rose to play her part in the great scheme of history. Meanwhile, in Jerusalem, the good king Hezekiah was succeeded by his wicked son Manasseh, who reigned for fifty-five years from 697 to 642 B.C.

Again the hills and valleys of Judah reeked with the smoke of heathen altars. Opposers were slain, the prophet Isaiah being one of the first to fall. Of Manasseh we read:

> He made his son pass through the fire, and observed times, and used enchantments, and dwelt with familiar spirits and wizards: he wrought much wickedness in the sight of the Lord, to provoke him to anger (2 Kings 21:6).

Significantly, the Assyrian tablets speak of that particular period as a time when great prominence was given to demonic phenomena, magic, divination, necromancy, and every variety of occultism. Speaking of the widespread use of such phenomena, William Hallo and William Simpson of Yale University write:

> Of all the manifestations of learned speculation in Mesopotamia, the most characteristic was divination. It reflected the official world view, as espoused by court and temple, as well as the popular belief of the masses. Beginning with scattered allusions in Sumerian sources, it developed into the largest single category of Akkadian literature in terms of sheer numbers of texts. A staggering number and variety of techniques, each with its own exhaustive handbooks, became a distinguishing mark of later Akkadian culture both in Mesopotamia and wherever that culture was exported, imitated, or even ridiculed abroad.[4]

No other period has yielded such a mass of tablets relating to magic and divination as the period of Judah's late history. Little wonder that King Manasseh succumbed to it.

Through the occult, Judah was led into complete apostasy, resulting in her captivity into Babylon. Judah's fate speaks forcefully about the dangers inherent in the occult explosion of our day.

Manasseh was followed by his evil son, Amon, who reigned only two years before he was slain by his servants. Then began the thirty-one-year reign of good king Josiah from about 640 to 609 B.C.

Seal rings bear witness

The youthful King Josiah cleansed the temple and brought about a much-needed revival and reformation. When the temple was being cleaned out, a great discovery was made. The Scripture reports, "Hilkiah the high priest said unto Shaphan the scribe, I have found the book of the law in the house of the Lord" (2 Kings 22:8).

In 1984, a seal ring belonging to the son of Hilkiah the priest was found in the home of an antique collector in Paris. The inscription on the ring reads, "(Belonging) to Hanan, son (of) Hilkiah, the priest."[5]

What a remarkable confirmation of the accuracy of Bible history!

Josiah was succeeded by Jehoiakim (609-598 B.C.), who became a vassal of Babylon, and as a result the reformation under Hezekiah was short-lived.

The prophet Jeremiah, who lived during these declining years of Judah, warned of coming disaster and tried to lead the people back to God. King Jehoiakim had him put into a dungeon. The prophet responded with a message of entreaty to the king that he had Baruch, his faithful companion and scribe, read to him. But the king cut the message in pieces and threw it in the fire.

A clay seal, or bulla, bearing the message in Hebrew, "Belonging to Baruch, son of Neriah, the Scribe," was discovered in Jerusalem. It was found in a hoard of bullae that first began to surface in an Arab antiquities shop in Jerusalem in 1975. The number grew to over 250. Although their origin remains a mystery, the dating is certain because of the biblical names on them.[6]

One of them bore the inscription, "Belonging to Jerahmeel, son of the king." Jerahmeel and others were commanded to capture Jeremiah and Baruch, "but the Lord hid them" (Jeremiah 36:26).

Another seal reads, "Belonging to Elishama, servant of the king." Elishama, the scribe, is referred to in Jeremiah 36:12.

The words of the prophet Jeremiah were read in the chamber of "Gemariah the son of Shaphan the scribe" (Jeremiah 36:10). A clay bulla bearing the name "Gemaryahu, son of Shaphan" was one of fifty-one such bullae found in the excavations of Ophel, the city of David, by Yigal Shiloh. The bullae were baked hard when the Babylonians put Jerusalem to the torch in 586 B.C.[7]

So, one after another, names familiar from the Bible have come to light in recent years, producing a striking confirmation of the biblical records.

Nebuchadnezzar's first campaign

According to the Bible, Nebuchadnezzar led three campaigns against Jerusalem. And all three have been confirmed in Babylonian texts.

The first campaign was in 605 B.C. when King Nabopolasser asked his young son, Nebuchadnezzar, to go west to meet the forces of Pharaoh-Necho of Egypt. As a result, Pharaoh-Necho was defeated in the famous Battle of Carchemish.

After the battle, as his army marched southward, Nebuchadnezzar received word that his father had died. Taking the shortest route possible, he hastened back to Babylon and assumed the throne.

Meanwhile, his armies invaded Palestine, where they laid siege to Jerusalem and took captives. Daniel and his three companions were among those captured and were carried back to Babylon.

In 1955, a small tablet surfaced that gives Nebuchadnezzar's own account of this campaign. The tablet was one of nine composing the Babylonian Chronicles, published by Donald J. Wiseman, a professor of Assyriology at the University of London since 1961. The nine tablets were among some ninety thousand that had lain unrecorded in the British Museum since sometime between 1872 and 1889.

One of the nine clay tablets supplies actual dates for events mentioned in the Bible. It speaks of the fall of Nineveh in 612 B.C. It also tells of Nebuchadnezzar's great victory at the Battle of Carchemish in 605 B.C. It reports his father's death on August 15 and tells how he hastened to Babylon and assumed the throne on September 7.

Although Jerusalem is not named in this first campaign of Nebuchadnezzar, it must have been included, for the text states that at that time Nebuchadnezzar "conquered all of Hatti-land [Syria-Palestine]."

The text of the tablets also says that after sacking a city, possibly Jerusalem (the name of the city is not readable), the armies went south and took Ashkelon. A fascinating letter relating to this campaign was found at Saqqara in Egypt in 1942. Written by Adon, who was apparently the king of the city-state of Ekron, a sister city near Ashkelon at the time, this letter is an appeal to Egypt for help. Nebuchadnezzar's troops were already as far south as Aphek—they would soon be at Ashkelon, and without help Adon would be unable to withstand the onslaught. Evidently the help never came, for Ashkelon fell.

The extent of this campaign is also indicated in the biblical record, which states: "The king of Babylon had taken from the river of Egypt unto the river Euphrates all that pertained to the king of Egypt" (2 Kings 24:7).

Nebuchadnezzar's second campaign

The Babylonian Chronicle recording Nebuchadnezzar's first campaign against Jerusalem is a little tablet as small as the palm of a hand. But in addition to giving details of his first campaign, the same tablet also speaks in graphic detail of Nebuchadnezzar's second campaign against Jerusalem.

The siege began on December 18, 598 B.C., and continued until March 16, 597 B.C., when the city capitulated. The tablet reads:

> In the seventh year, in the month of Kislev, the Babylonian king mustered his troops, and, having marched to the land of Hatti, besieged the city of Judah, and on the second day of the month of Adar took the city and captured the king. He appointed therein a king of his own choice, received its heavy tribute and sent (them) to Babylon.[8]

The Bible is in complete agreement with the Babylonian text. It reports that Jehoiachin, the king in Jerusalem, was taken captive to Babylon, and that King Zedekiah was installed in Jerusalem as a puppet ruler (see 2 Kings 24:15, 17).

This text also states that the king's mother and the king's wives and his officers were taken captive with Jehoiachin (see 2 Kings 24:15).

During the excavations of Babylon by Robert Koldeway (1899-1917), a hoard of three hundred dated tablets were found near the Ishtar Gate. They lay undisturbed in the Berlin Museum until published by Ernest Weidner in the late 1930s. But they did not become known by British and American scholars until after World War II.

One of the tablets, dated 592 B.C., includes a record of the rations given to the prisoners taken to Babylon. Weidner, while studying the text, suddenly came across the name of "Yaukin [Jehoiachin], king of Yahud [Judah]." An exact parallel to 2 Kings 24:15, 17, Jehoiachin's rations were twenty times that of any of the others, obviously enough to provide for those with him—his mother, wives and family, along with leading officials. Again we have striking confirmation of the accurate details of the biblical account.

The final assault

The Babylonian Chronicles end with the year 593 B.C., so

the final campaign of 589-586 B.C. is not included. However, an inscription believed by some scholars to refer to this campaign was discovered by workmen who were engaged in repairs on an old aqueduct on the shores of the Nahr el-Kelb (Dog River) north of Beirut. On the stone bank they recognized some ancient writing that, upon examination, was understood to refer to Nebuchadnezzar's third campaign into Palestine, although the name of Jerusalem is not discernible.

Remarkable evidence of this destruction was uncovered during the excavations of Ophel by Yigal Shiloh, begun in 1978 and concluded as a result of his death in 1987. His excavations uncovered remains of three houses of the eighth and seventh centuries B.C. that show dramatic evidence of the conflagration by fire. Ahiel's house is so named because his name was found in it. The House of Bullae is so called because of the fifty-one clay bullae, or seals, found within. The third house is called the Burnt Room. It is covered with a thick layer of dark ash and contains carbonized remnants of decorated wood furniture and wood ceiling beams, as well as a dagger and mason's hammer. Scores of bronze and iron arrowheads were discovered nearby, bringing to life the fierce struggle that occurred.[9]

Excavations at the fortress city of Lachish, about eighteen miles southwest of Jerusalem, have also produced striking evidence of Nebuchadnezzar's presence. There is clear proof that the city was burned twice over a short period of time, coinciding with Nebuchadnezzar's campaigns of 597 and 586 B.C. A clay seal found within the debris bears the inscription, "The property of Gedaliah who is over the house." In 2 Kings 25:22 we are told: "As for the people that remained in the land of Judah, whom Nebuchadnezzar king of Babylon had left, even over them he made Gedaliah . . . ruler."

Also of special interest was the discovery of twenty-one pieces of pottery that had messages inscribed on them. Most of them were hasty notes asking for help written by the commander of the Judean forces near Lachish. Known as the

Lachish Letters, letter 4 reads in part, "And [my lord] will know that we are watching for the signals of Lachish, according to all signs which my Lord hath given, for we cannot see Azekah."[10]

Apparently, the city of Azekah had already fallen, for it was no longer sending its smoke signals. Lachish was sure to be next, and these letters were a frantic appeal for help.

The very same situation is vividly described in Jeremiah 34:7:

When the king of Babylon's army fought against Jerusalem, and against all the cities of Judah that were left, against Lachish, and against Azekah: for these defenced cities remained of the cities of Judah.

After Azekah fell, only Lachish was left. Soon it was taken, and then Jerusalem was reduced to complete ruin. Its inhabitants, except for a small remnant, were taken as captives to Babylon.

---

1. Finegan, *Light From the Ancient Past*, 180.

2. Ibid.

3. *The Baghdad Observer*, 6 June 1990.

4. William W. Hallo and William Kelly Simpson, *The Ancient Near East—a History* (New York: Harcourt Brace Jovanovich, 1971), 158.

5. Josette Elayi, "Name of Deuteronomy's Author Found on Seal Ring," *BAR*, September/October 1987, 54-56.

6. Hershel Shanks, "Jeremiah's Scribe and Confidant Speaks From a Hoard of Clay Bullae," *BAR*, September/October 1987, 58-65.

7. Hershel Shanks, "The City of David After Five Years of Digging," *BAR*, November/December 1985, 22-38.

8. D. Winton Thomas, ed., *Documents From Old Testament Times* (New York: Harper and Row, 1961), 80.

9. Shanks, "The City of David After Five Years of Digging," *BAR*, November/December 1985, 30-32.

10. Thomas, *Documents From Old Testament Times*, 216.

Chapter 20

Babylon—the Glory of Kingdoms

Following the fall of the Assyrian Empire, Babylon became the master of the Old World.

Our taxi sped across the Mesopotamian desert toward the mound of the ancient city of Babylon, fifty-five miles south of Baghdad. It was a miserably hot day in July. The lonesome miles of barren landscape gave little reminder of what had once been the "garden of God." The great system of canals and ditches that had once been a major industry had long since gone to ruin.

The monotony was broken as we pulled up to a conspicuous mound rising from the dust to the right of the highway. Here the great King Nebuchadnezzar had built his summer palace. Trailing off into the distance, an ancient embankment indicated where the walls of his city had been.

A few more miles, and we arrived at the greater mound of the inner city. The path up the slope was next to a small building housing a mini-museum. Continuing beyond the museum to the top of the mound, then looking to the left, we saw the spot where the great Ishtar Gate had been exposed by archaeologists. On either side, as far as our eyes could see, were heaping mounds of ruins and partially exposed walls and chambers.

The excavations of Babylon were under the direction of German archaeologist Robert Koldewey, who dug there for eighteen years from 1899 to 1917, in one of the most massive archaeological projects ever undertaken.

The Ishtar Gateway, 170 feet long, had been exposed to a height of forty feet. Its great walls were richly adorned with creatures of blue glazed tile, decorated with yellow and other sparkling hues. Although the tile had all been removed, the forms of dragons, lions, and other animals were still clearly visible.

We walked along the broad Procession Street, seventy-five feet wide, partially excavated. On this sacred street the images of the gods were carried during the New Year festival. One side of each of the large bricks bore the inscription: "Nebuchadnezzar, king of Babylon, provider of Esagila and Ezida, first born son of Nabopolasser, king of Babylon."

The German archaeologists assumed the enormous task of removing the glazed tiles from the gateway, carting them to Germany, and restoring the gate to near its original size in the famous Pergamon Museum in Berlin. They covered it with the original glazed tile, making it possible to see the Ishtar Gate as Daniel himself saw it more than 2,500 years ago when he went about his official business for the king.

Seven gateways led into the city, four of which were excavated by Koldewey, the Ishtar Gate being the principal one. A smaller version of a Babylonian gateway, decorated with ornamental lions, all of the original tile, occupies a prominent position in the Oriental Institute Museum of Chicago.

The lion was a principal symbol of Babylon. On the Ishtar Processional Way there are sixty lions alternating with sixty bulls. The front wall of the Ishtar Gate is adorned with bulls and dragons, a composite beast. On the outer wall of the throne room in the courtyard of the palace, only lions appear. We can readily understand why in the prophecy of Daniel 7, the lion is used to represent the ancient nation.

Walking across the ruin and rubble, we came to the spot where the famous tower of Babylon once stood, perhaps the original Tower of Babel of biblical fame. It is now a depression partially filled with water. The tower once stood in a sacred complex occupying some sixty acres. It was a sort of Babylonian Vatican, the religious center of the vast empire.

As we looked over the vast desolation, it was hard to imagine that this city had once been the most magnificent and glorious city of the ancient world. What Nebuchadnezzar inherited from his father, Nabopolasser, was only a mile square. Then Nebuchadnezzar enlarged it to a circumference of ten miles. This compared well with other ancient cities. Nineveh was eight and a half miles around, imperial Rome six, and Athens but four.

The inner city was surrounded by double walls twelve and twenty-two feet wide, respectively, and outer double walls twenty-four and twenty-six feet wide. Inner walls also lined the Euphrates River that ran through the city. The space between the walls was sometimes filled, allowing space at the top wide enough for four span of horses. Every 160 feet, huge watchtowers rose above the walls.

Describing the construction of the walls, Nebuchadnezzar wrote,

> "I caused a mighty wall to circumscribe Babylon in the east. I dug its moats; and its escarpments I built out of bitumen and kiln brick. At the edge of the moat I built a powerful wall as high as a hill. I gave it wide gates and set in doors of cedarwood sheathed with copper."[1]

The truth about Nebuchadnezzar

Scholars used to question whether Nebuchadnezzar was really the great builder and king set forth in the book of Daniel. The city, they argued, was probably the work of Semiramis of Greek legendary fame. Now they know differently.

Thousands of inscribed tablets, clay cylinders, and construction bricks were found at Babylon, most of them relating to Nebuchadnezzar, thousands of them stamped with his name. In some of the foundations the excavators found deposits of clay cylinders that described the buildings. Because of these excavations, we know more about Nebuchadnezzar than about any other ancient king. And today, all scholars agree that he was one of the greatest kings who ever lived and one of the greatest builders of all time. Again the Bible has been vindicated in a remarkable way.

Concerning the original tower, Nabopolasser wrote:

"The Lord Marduk commanded me concerning Etemenanki, the stepped tower of Babylon, which before my time had fallen into decay and ruin, to establish its foundation in the heart of the underworld and make its summit like the heavens."[2]

When Nebuchadnezzar completed the restoration, he wrote:

All the peoples of many nations . . . I put to work on the building of Etemenanki. . . . The high dwelling of Marduk my Lord I placed at its summit. . . . I beautified the pinnacle of Etemenanki with splendid bricks of blue enamel.[3]

Many of the inscriptions have a direct relationship to the book of Daniel. In Daniel 4:30 we read, "The king spake, and said, Is not this great Babylon, that I have built for the house of the kingdom by the might of my power, and for the honour of my majesty?"

In the Royal Ontario Museum in Canada I spied a clay cylinder on which Nebuchadnezzar declares, "Let the learned read again and again all my deeds which I have written in my inscription, and let him ever give thought to the praise I deserve from the gods."

The words almost seem to come right out of the book of Daniel.

Nabonidus and Belshazzar

According to the fifth chapter of Daniel, Belshazzar was king of Babylon when the city fell. But this posed a problem that the critics eagerly seized upon. According to the Babylonian inscriptions, Nabonidus was the king at that time. There was, in fact, no record outside of the Bible that a king with the name Belshazzar had ever lived. So critics had a field day. Whole books were written to disprove the book of Daniel, using this nonexistent king as the chief argument.

Then in 1861, for the first time, the name Belshazzar appeared on a Babylonian text. In 1882, the now famous Chronicle of Nabonidus came to light. It stated that Nabonidus, Belshazzar's father, was in Tema during his final years and his son was in Babylon. The name of Nabonidus's son, or the position he held, was not given in the Chronicle of Nabonidus. But in 1884, another tablet named Belshazzar as the son of Nabonidus. And on an inscription initially read in 1916, Nabonidus and Belshazzar are named jointly in an oath. The crowning evidence came to light in 1924 on an inscription in which King Nabonidus declares, "I entrusted kingship on my son Belshazzar."

Today, due to the many cylinders, tablets, and other inscriptions mentioning Nabonidus, he has become a familiar figure. As an old man, he spent his last years in retirement in Tema in Arabia, leaving the actual kingship to his son, Belshazzar, who reigned as coregent.

These records help to explain Daniel 5:29, which places Daniel as "the third ruler in the kingdom." Nabonidus was first, Belshazzar second, and Daniel third.

Although problems with the biblical record may appear, sometimes after long years of waiting, evidence eventually comes to light that shows that the Bible is right after all.

The Cyrus Cylinder and the Bible

Perhaps the most significant inscription to be found in Babylon was the Cyrus Cylinder discovered in 1887. On it,

Cyrus gives his own account of how he took the city of Babylon. According to this cylinder, Marduk pronounced Cyrus as the one destined to rule the world; it records how Babylon was taken without a battle and how Cyrus was welcomed by the people; then how by royal edict the captives in Babylon were released and permitted to return to their own lands and rebuild their sanctuaries.

Much of the remarkable text of the Cyrus Cylinder can be correlated with the Bible, particularly with the prophecy of Isaiah. According to Isaiah, God ordained that Cyrus would be the one to take the city of Babylon, free the Jewish captives, and aid them in restoring their temple.

Notice the amazing prophecy of Isaiah, made about 150 years before Cyrus invaded Babylon. In this prophecy God is speaking. He says:

> That saith to the deep, Be dry, and I will dry up thy rivers: That saith of Cyrus, He is my shepherd, and shall perform all my pleasure: even saying to Jerusalem, Thou shalt be built; and to the temple, Thy foundation shall be laid. Thus saith the Lord to his anointed, to Cyrus, whose right hand I have holden, to subdue nations before him; and I will loose the loins of kings, to open before him the two leaved gates; and the gates shall not be shut (Isaiah 44:27–45:1).

According to Herodotus, and in a dramatic fulfillment of this prophecy, Cyrus had the Euphrates River, which ran diagonally through the city, diverted into an artificial lake. He then marched his men along the river bottom into the city and through the inner "leaved" gates that had been carelessly left open. Cyrus was welcomed by the people as their deliverer and installed as their ruler.

Daniel 5:29 names Darius the Mede as the king of this new empire. Darius may have been Gabaru, the general who conquered Babylon for Cyrus, and may have served briefly as vassal king under Cyrus. In any event, he died shortly after the conquest, and Cyrus served as the supreme sovereign. He then issued the decree permitting the Jews to return to Jerusalem and rebuild their sanctuary (Ezra 1).

Here are the words of Cyrus:

> I returned to (these) sacred cities on the other side of the Tigris, the sanctuaries of which have been in ruins for a long time, the images which (used) to live therein and established for them permanent sanctuaries. I (also) gathered all their (former) inhabitants and returned (to them) their habitations.[4]

Of Cyrus, the prophet Isaiah declares,

> I have raised him up in righteousness, and I will direct all his ways: he shall build my city, and he shall let go my captives, not for price nor reward, saith the Lord of hosts (Isaiah 45:13).

Jeremiah had foretold that the Jews would be in Babylon for seventy years (see Jeremiah 25:11). At the end of the seventy years, God raised up Cyrus to bring about their release. What is most remarkable about this prophecy is that the words of Isaiah were written more than a century before Cyrus was born.

Fulfilled prophecy is one of the greatest evidences that the Bible is a divinely inspired book. But Bible critics, unwilling to accept the prophetic aspect of the Bible, attempt to find some other explanation.

In this case, they proposed that the book of Isaiah is the work of two authors—that the prophetic part, from chapter 40 on, was written some centuries after the events occurred by a later, unknown forger.

But then came the discovery in 1947 of the Dead Sea Scrolls, most of them dating from the second and first centuries B.C. The most famous among them was the Isaiah scroll—the complete book of Isaiah. From it, it is evident that the scholars of that day regarded the book of Isaiah as the work of a single author. There is no evidence of any break in the text between chapters 39 and 40. Clearly, Isaiah was regarded as the work of a single author when the canon of Scripture was established in the last centuries preceding the Christian era. It was also regarded as the work of a single author by Christ and the New Testament writers who quote from it. And it was so regarded by the early church fathers. The Christian church regarded all of Isaiah as the work of a single author and a part of the canon of Scripture until the rise of the higher critical school in Germany in the nineteenth century. And the Dead Sea Scrolls have weakened the attack of these critics. The prophecy of Isaiah about Cyrus confirms the historical accuracy and divine inspiration of the Word of God.

---

1. C. W. Ceram, *Gods, Graves, and Scholars* (New York: Alfred A. Knopf, 1954), 284.
2. André Parrot, *Babylon and the Old Testament* (New York Philosophical Library, 1958), 49.
3. Ibid.
4. Pritchard, *The Ancient Near East*, 208.

Chapter 21

Daniel in the Critics' Den

We know that God delivered Daniel from the lions' den. But how has he fared in the critics' den? The book of Daniel has probably been the object of more criticism than any other book in the Bible.

Higher critics of the nineteenth century resurrected the idea first advanced by Porphyry in the third century A.D. that the book of Daniel was written by some unknown Jew in the time of Antiochus Epiphanes about 165 B.C., and that it was not really the work of Daniel.

With the discovery of the Dead Sea Scrolls at Qumran the critics were dealt a telling blow, for the book of Daniel was among the most popular books, with at least eight copies found among them, four of them from Cave IV.

Was Daniel really the great hero of Babylon? A scroll fragment from Cave IV known as the Florilegium, a sort of commentary, refers to "the writings of Daniel the prophet." It also refers to "the writings of Isaiah the prophet" and of "Ezekiel the prophet." Obviously, Daniel was fully accepted as a prophet by the writers and the custodians of the scrolls, as were Isaiah and Ezekiel.

Josephus, the Jewish historian of the first century A.D., furnishes additional evidence that the book of Daniel was written in the sixth century B.C. He records that after Alexander the Great fought the Battle of Tyre in 331 B.C., he went down to Jerusalem, where he was shown the book of

Daniel. Alexander recognized himself as the Greek in Daniel's prophecy who would conquer the Persians. If the critics' late date for Daniel were correct, the collapse of Persia would have taken place 166 years before they said the book of Daniel was written. Since this is of course an impossibility, the critics were proved wrong, and the authenticity of the book of Daniel is again established.

The evidence mounts. The critics had contended that the portions of the book of Daniel written in Aramaic, chapters 2:4 to 7:28, belonged to the Maccabean period of the second century B.C.* But we now have the witness of the Elephantine Papyri. These manuscripts were found in Egypt on the island of Elephantine, opposite Aswan, where a colony of Jews, most of them mercenary soldiers, had been stationed.

Shortly after the find, the manuscripts were purchased by a Mr. Wilbur in 1893. He died at sea, however, on his way back to America. His trunk containing the manuscripts was stored in a warehouse in New York City and remained unopened for fifty years. When it came into possession of the Brooklyn museum, the documents were read by Dr. Emil Kraeling, who at once recognized their importance.

The Elephantine Papyri belong to the period of Ezra and Nehemiah of the fifth century B.C. They are now considered an indispensable aid in the study of the customs and international relations of that time. They are written in Aramaic, the language that corresponds more closely to the Aramaic portions of the book of Daniel than to that of the Maccabean period. Thus further evidence of the earlier authorship of Daniel is provided.

The book of Daniel was written by the prophet Daniel in the time of Babylon. We can truly depend on the historical accuracy of the Bible!

Babylon in Bible prophecy

Not only has the early dating of the book of Daniel been firmly established, but also the amazing accuracy of its prophecies, which trace the rise and fall of empires.

The present desolation of Babylon also provides a striking fulfillment of ancient prophecies. When the city was still in its heyday as the wonder of the ancient world, the prophet Jeremiah daringly predicted:

> Babylon shall become heaps, a dwelling place for dragons, an astonishment, and an hissing, without an inhabitant. . . . The broad walls of Babylon shall be utterly broken (Jeremiah 51:37, 58).

And Isaiah foretold,

> Babylon, the glory of kingdoms, the beauty of the Chaldees' excellency, shall be as when God overthrew Sodom and Gomorrah. It shall never be inhabited, neither shall it be dwelt in from generation to generation (Isaiah 13:19, 20).

What a striking fulfillment of the prophecies as we look over the desolation and ruin of Babylon today! The prophets foretold that the city would be overthrown and left "without an inhabitant," that its broad walls would be broken down, that it would be a desolation. History has shown how remarkably well the prophecy was fulfilled.

But something has happened to Babylon in recent years. A great restoration project has been underway, one of the boldest ever attempted. From 22 September to 22 October 1987, Saddam Hussein and the Iraqi government sponsored an event to celebrate the completion of the first phase of the project, the first of an annual International Festival of Babylon.

While attending the festival, I was impressed by the amazing change that had occurred since my earlier visit thirty years before. The fifty-five mile drive from Baghdad is now along a modern superhighway. Near the approach to Babylon, a monumental gateway stands. From there a broad, tree-lined boulevard leads to the restored part of the city.

I entered the part of the city under restoration by way of a half-size reproduction of the Ishtar Gate, this about a half mile from the original site. Walking through a large courtyard, I followed a path that leads up to a broad avenue. From the avenue, I viewed heaps of ruins and partially exposed walls and chambers, a witness to the excavations of Koldewey.

On the left, I entered a restored complex of huge doorways and chambers identified as a part of the Southern Palace of King Nebuchadnezzar. A short hike across the rubble of ancient remains took me to a second restored structure—the throne room of the king, the most auspicious of the 250 rooms that had comprised the ancient palace. It was filled with chairs, and technicians were at work setting up equipment for a cultural program scheduled for the evening.

Gazing about, I could scarcely believe that I was standing in what is believed to have been the festival hall of Belshazzar. Here the king was no doubt engaged in the great feast with "a thousand of his lords" the night the mysterious writing spelling his doom appeared on the surrounding walls (see Daniel 5:1).

The year subsequent to my visit saw the walls and gateways leading into the palace also restored, along with additional rooms and courts, all restored on the foundations of the original structures. Inside the main entrance are five restored courtyards surrounded by administrative buildings. Here, close by the throne room, Daniel must have carried on his official duties for the king.

Back on the broad avenue, I soon approached the historic Ishtar Gate. Its original walls, to a height of forty or more feet, still stand, decorated with characteristic lion, bull, and dragon reliefs. Even with the decorative glazed tile removed, the animal reliefs are still clearly visible.

I followed the broad stairway down into the 170-foot-long gateway. The gateway at this level, along with the present walls, is the work of Nabopolasser. Nebuchadnezzar erected a new gateway above the work of his father. Nebuchadnezzar's work consisted of two massive gates that served as the principal entry into the inner city. It was the tile from these gates that was removed by the German archaeologists and placed on the reconstructed, almost full-size gateway in the Pergomon Museum in Berlin—one of the most amazing museum displays on earth.

Steps at the far end of the gateway took me again to the street level of Nebuchadnezzar. I had now entered upon the sacred Procession Street, seventy feet wide and fully restored. Daniel and his fellow captives would no doubt have been brought into the city along this pavement, the principal entry into the inner city via the Ishtar Gate. The massive walls that stood on either side of the Procession Street had been restored for the distance of a quarter of a mile, pierced by occasional colossal doorways.

I also visited the restored E-mah Temple of Nebuchadnezzar, a massive structure that stands on the opposite side of the avenue fronting the Southern Palace. It was also used as the stage for cultural performances during the International Festival of Babylon.

Posters advertising the International Festival had as its theme "From Nebuchadnezzar to Saddam Hussein—Babylon undergoes a renaissance." Saddam Hussein has grandiose plans for the restoration of the ancient Babylonian Empire and characterizes himself as the new Nebuchadnezzar. Just what the future will bring in the light of the disastrous One Hundred–Hour War of January 1991 is uncertain.

But the question naturally arises, Do these restorations nullify the prophecies? Not at all. The vast area of Nebuchadnezzar's city remains, for the most part, a ruin and a desolation, as described by the prophets. A small portion has been reconstructed to constitute a great open-air museum. But there are no inhabitants.

I arrived at the entrance gate at nine o'clock in the morning, armed with a special pass provided by the Department of Antiquities, and spent several hours on the site. The doors for the festival would not be officially opened until 4:00 p.m., so I had the place to myself. The only people I saw were three or four police officers and a few men working on the grounds.

The prophecies are still true. The Bible is 100 percent trustworthy. Babylon for the most part is still in ruins. The city remains without an inhabitant. My hope is that as tourists come to stand, look, and marvel, they will be led to a study of the book of Daniel and its messages for our day. Thanks to the work of the archaeologists, Daniel can be accepted with complete confidence.

---

* Two fragments of the book of Daniel from Qumran cover Daniel 2:4 and 7:28, where the language changes occur, and the change is present in both of the fragments.

Chapter 22

Jerusalem in the Time of Christ

Jerusalem means "city of peace," but the city has been the seat of unending strife. Following its destruction by King Nebuchadnezzar and the Babylonians in 586 B.C., Jerusalem lay in utter ruin, and the most noble of the land were taken captive into Babylon.

After seventy years of captivity in Babylon, Cyrus the Persian issued a decree granting the captives permission to return to Jerusalem and rebuild their temple. Encouraged by the prophets Haggai and Zechariah, and under the strong leadership of Zerubbabel, the work began. When opposition brought the work to a halt, a second decree was issued in 520 B.C. by Darius the Great.

Finally, under the provisions of a third decree, issued by Artaxerxes in 457 B.C., and under the capable leadership of Nehemiah, assisted by Ezra, the work was completed. Some scholars have contested 457 B.C. as the year of this third decree, opting instead for 458. Which year is correct depends on which calendar was being used at that time. The Elephantine Papyri have proven the year 457 to be correct.

The date 457 B.C. is significant, for it is the key in Daniel's prophecy of the seventy weeks that establishes the exact date for the appearance of the Messiah. Jesus was baptized, began His ministry, and died on the cross at the precise time foretold in the prophecy (see Daniel 9:25, 27). Little wonder that Daniel's prophecy is recognized as the most significant prophecy in the Bible, for it gives indisputable evidence that Jesus was indeed the true Messiah foretold in the Old Testament Scriptures.

After Babylon fell, under the Persians and then under Alexander the Great of Greece, the Jews were treated with great consideration. When Alexander died, the Greek Empire was divided among his four leading generals. Since Palestine came under the portion of the divided Greek Empire controlled by the Ptolemies of Egypt, the Jews had nothing to fear.

But the picture changed dramatically after 198 B.C. when Antiochus III of Syria gained control of Palestine by defeating the Egyptians in the battle of Paneas (Banias, the Caesarea Phillipi of the New Testament). His son subsequently tried to force the Jews to worship the Greek gods.

When Antiochus IV, who is often called Antiochus Epiphanes, became king, he put forth an all-out effort to abolish all Jewish customs and religion. A Greek gymnasium was erected in Jerusalem, Greek customs introduced, and pagan shrines set up throughout the country. To top it off, the worship of Jehovah was abolished from the Jewish temple and a statue of the Olympian god Zeus was installed. The desecration of the temple resulted in the Maccabean revolt.

After the death of Antiochus Epiphanes, a truce was proclaimed, and the city of Jerusalem was divided. The Jews were now permitted to restore their temple and its services. On 25 December 165 B.C., just three years after the temple was desecrated by a statue of the god Zeus, the golden candlesticks were again lighted. At Christmastime, the Jewish celebration of Hanukkah, the Festival of Lights, is in celebration of this victory of the Maccabees.

The Jews enjoyed their independence during the century that followed. But in 63 B.C., when Pompey besieged Jerusalem, twelve thousand Jews were slain, and the city was made subject to Rome.

In 40 B.C., Herod the Great was named king of Judea by the

Roman Senate. Since he was so hated by the Jews, it was three years before he was able to gain the throne. His last battle was fought in Jerusalem, where it took the Romans three months to take the upper city and the temple site.

Herod, the master builder

Herod became one of the ancient world's master builders. One of his first projects as king of Judea was at Caesarea on the Palestinian coast. There he built a magnificent city as his capital. It took between ten and twelve years to build, the dedication occurring in 12 B.C. The province of Judea, and later, the province of Syria-Palestine, was governed from Caesarea for six hundred years, until the Muslim conquest of the seventh century.

Caesarea was a port city, built along a forty-mile stretch of inhospitable coastline without any natural haven for ships. But the ambitious king built a harbor there that became one of the three largest ports of the ancient world, rivaling even that of Athens.

He constructed a massive breakwater more than two hundred feet wide, a third of a mile into the sea. Josephus tells us that Herod used blocks of stone fifty feet long, eighteen feet wide, and ten feet high, let down into water 120 feet deep. The breakwater and mole have long since been destroyed, but it is still possible to see their outline from an airplane overhead.

Underwater biblical archaeology began in 1960 with the exploration of a Phoenician shipwreck off the coast of Turkey. That same year, underwater explorations of the Caesarea harbor installations also began, a project that continued with only occasional breaks until 1979.

The harbor represents one of the engineering marvels of the world and a mastery of technology rivaling our own age. A high-quality concrete was used that hardened under water and was practically unaffected by the destructive action of the sea.

Caesarea was a magnificent city beside this harbor and

covered some 164 acres. The city was under excavation for more than a decade. A principal attraction is the great Roman amphitheater, restored and used today for cultural performances. A prime discovery at Caesarea was a slab of stone found near the entrance to the amphitheater, bearing the name of Pontius Pilate—before whom Jesus was brought to trial. The inscription reads, "Pontius Pilate, the prefect of Judea, has dedicated to the people of Caesarea a temple in honor of Tiberias."

A temple to Mithra was found in one of the large underground vaults that are near the amphitheater. Although more than eight hundred Mithrean temples are known in various parts of Europe and North Africa, this is the first one found in Palestine. The hippodrome, 1,500 feet long and 250 feet wide, was also discovered. It was used for athletic events, including the Roman chariot races. Within it stood an obelisk, seventy-two feet tall.

Caesarea and the Jews

The Jews were in constant conflict with the Romans, who had their principal army garrisons at Caesarea. Jerusalem was divided into separate sections for the Jews, the Samaritans, and the Greeks. When a disagreement broke out in regard to access by the Jews to a synagogue in one of the Gentile sections of the city, it was misinterpreted by the Jewish community in Caesarea. They understood it to mean that Roman soldiers from Caesarea had tried to put down a Jewish insurrection in Jerusalem and had plundered the temple treasury. The Caesarean Jews reacted with an attack on the Roman garrison in Caesarea. The Roman troops under Vespasian responded, killing twenty thousand Jews, most of them in the Caesarean hippodrome.

When Vespasian became emperor of Rome, Titus, operating with supplies from Caesarea, led the final assault on Jerusalem. In A.D. 70, after a five-month siege, Jerusalem was captured and the temple burned, as we will see in more detail later. Titus returned to Caesarea with Jewish captives, and, to celebrate his victory, 2,500 Jews were put to death in gladiatorial combats and by wild beasts in the amphitheater.

An arch was erected in Rome to commemorate the victory. Known as the Arch of Titus, reliefs on it depict the taking of the seven-branched candlesticks and other sacred objects from the temple. A Roman coin was also struck to celebrate the victory.

Herod also constructed a huge aqueduct that brought water into Caesarea from springs near the foot of Mount Carmel, twelve miles away. The water was carried first through a tunnel six miles long, cut through the limestone rock of Carmel; it connected with an elevated aqueduct six and a half miles long. So Caesarea was supplied with water from an aqueduct nearly thirteen miles long. A long portion of the elevated aqueduct still stands and is in a remarkable state of preservation.

Caesarea is mentioned several times in the New Testament. Philip, one of the seven evangelists sent out from Jerusalem, made his home here and no doubt became the leader of the first Christian church here (see Acts 8:40). Peter came to Caesarea on his visit to Cornelius, who became the first Gentile convert to Christianity (see Acts 10).

A landmark of the area is an ancient Crusader castle hugging the seashore. Somewhere in this area the apostle Paul was imprisoned during his two years in Caesarea, on his way to Rome.

Caesarea after A.D. 70

Following the destruction of Jerusalem in A.D. 70 and another crushing Jewish revolt sixty years later, Caesarea continued as the capital and chief city of Palestine. Subsequently, it became the capital of the Roman province of Syria-Palestine. The city continued to grow in size and importance during the second, third, and fourth centuries. It was the home of several prominent "fathers" of the Christian church.

Origen, the Greek theologian, taught here for twenty-three years. He established a major library. Eusebius, the father of church history, became the bishop of Caesarea in the fourth century A.D. In Origen's day, the famous library he founded contained thirty thousand volumes. When Constantine ordered fifty Bibles sent to the new churches of the empire, they were copied in the scriptorium of Caesarea.

In 640, Caesarea was captured by the Muslims as they went forth in their conquests of the Near East. After that, the city slowly declined, finally becoming a village. Its stone structures were used as a quarry for building other cities. Seven hundred Corinthian columns that lined the main street of the city were removed and placed under water to form a ramp over which the massive stones were loaded on ships bound for Acco.

In 1251, the crusaders occupied the site and built a city fortified with massive walls that still dominate the area. King Louis IX of France spent a full year restoring the city, often assisting in the actual work of construction.[1]

Josephus left a vivid description of the work of Herod at Caesarea, but scholars generally questioned whether his account was reliable. The archaeologists have proved Josephus to be correct.

Masada

Josephus also has much to say about the amazing fortress and palace King Herod built for himself on top of the 1,350-foot-high mountain of Masada on the western shores of the Dead Sea. Covering twenty-three acres, this lofty bastion was surrounded with a massive wall that was topped by thirty-seven watchtowers and became a landmark in the area.

Herod died in 4 B.C., leaving the fortress to a succession of Roman garrisons. When the Roman troops moved in to quell the Jewish rebellion in A.D. 69, a band of 960 Jewish zealots, under Eleazar ben Yair, retreated into this wilderness and occupied the then deserted citadel.

Safe in the fortress of Masada, the zealots defied the might of Rome for three long years. Then five thousand men of the tenth Roman Legion, commanded by Flavius Silva, the procurator of Judea, arrived on the scene with orders to wipe out the Jewish zealots. Siege engines and mobile catapults with a two-thousand-foot range were moved to the foot of the mountain. For seven months, rocks and balls of fire reigned down upon the besieged fortress. The siege continued from the autumn of A.D. 72 until the Passover in the spring of 73.

The besiegers established themselves in huge camps around the base of the mountain. Then they encircled the mountain with a massive stone wall so that none could escape.

The Romans, deciding finally to make a single massive assault, constructed a huge ramp, using the forced labor of thousands of sick and starving Jewish war prisoners. On it, they then moved up a siege tower equipped with catapults and a huge battering ram. After opening a breach in the wall, torch bearers rushed through, setting fires as they went. With victory assured, the Romans retired for the night and prepared for an all-out assault in the morning.

But what they found the next morning was far different from anything they could have anticipated. Josephus gives this graphic account. As the flames raced along Masada's ramparts, Eleazar ben Yair called the leaders of his besieged band together. He explained how they could choose an honorable death and leave this world unenslaved.

Responding to the challenge, the 960 zealots decided on mass suicide. Each man bade farewell to his wife and family, then killed them. Then ten men were chosen by lot to slay the other men. With only the ten men remaining, lots were cast among them and one was chosen to slay the other nine. This accomplished, the lone survivor set fire to the royal palace and with his full strength drove his sword into his own body.

The next morning, the Roman legion found only smoldering ruins, stark silence, and the bodies of the slain.

Two women with their five children had hidden themselves

in a cave and survived the slaughter. No doubt it was from them, as well as the Romans, that Josephus gained the information for his vivid account.

Yadin to the scene

Yigael Yadin, a professor of archaeology at Hebrew University, studied the Josephus account with unusual interest. He wondered if excavations of the site would confirm the almost incredible story, and what treasures might be hidden there.

In 1963, Yadin began two intensive, unforgettable, seven-month expeditions that would normally have taken twenty-five seasons. In his exciting volume *Masada*, he tells the amazing story.[2] He had the help of the Israeli Army Engineer Corps. Helicopters aided in the preliminary survey and in moving heavy equipment. They operated from a base camp of fifty tents. A cable was installed to haul up heavy supplies.

Advertisements for volunteer workers in the *Israeli Press* and London *Observer* brought five thousand responses from twenty-eight countries. Yadin's work was conducted in two-week shifts with three hundred workers at a time. The excavations continued from October 1963 to May 1964; then again, from November to April of 1965.

Today, Masada has become a vast open-air museum and a major tourist attraction. A visitor will long remember the suffocating heat as well as the importance of carrying drinking water.

The approach to the citadel is by either the Western Trail or the more lengthy, more winding Serpentine Trail on the east. More popular than either trail is the aerial cable car that runs from the restaurant and rest house on the east to the Eastern Gate at the summit.

The old Roman campsites are clearly visible from the trails, as are the remains of the great wall that once encircled the area. Guardrails offer protection from the steep, almost perpendicular slopes.

Exploring the evidence

The summit is surrounded with casemate walls—parallel walls with connecting walls between. Rooms on the wall served as the principal dwelling places for the patriots.

Within these rooms, Yadin found ample evidence of their being lived in by the zealots. On the floors were pieces of cloth that had been parts of bags and tunics. Cupboards were still stored with food left by the zealots—dates, walnuts, olive stones, salt, grain, and pomegranate seeds. Also found were cooking pots, pans, jugs, and scores of clay oil lamps belonging to the zealots. Even cosmetic equipment was found in the dwellings—palettes, bronze eye-shadow sticks, perfume vials, a mirror case, and a comb. There were also bronze objects such as belt buckles and key rings.

Near the Western Gate stands the Western Palace, partly reconstructed. From a walkway, one observes the various rooms that have been excavated. Of special interest is the well-preserved fifth-century mosaic that covered the palace floor, evidence that monks once inhabited the area. They lived here in cells until forced to vacate at the time of the seventh-century Muslim conquest.

A lengthy hike from the Western Palace, beneath the scorching sun, brings the weary but fascinated observer to the administrative buildings, the storerooms, and a chapel dating to Byzantine times. It consists mostly of a long hall with an apse at the end. The walls are preserved to a remarkable degree, still retaining some of the original plaster. The floor is enriched with a fifth-century mosaic.

Of still greater interest is the ancient synagogue. It seemed clear to Yadin that at least the benches were constructed by the zealots in the first century, thus making it a find of supreme importance in the field of Jewish archaeology. Up to this time, the earliest known synagogue was from the end of the second century or the beginning of the third century A.D. This one is probably 150 years older.

Of equal importance were the discoveries within the synagogue that included a large hoard of coins found on the floor, dating to the period of the Jewish revolt. Portions of fourteen scrolls, both biblical and nonbiblical, were also discovered. They are considered to be the most important find of the entire project.

The most exciting discovery, however, was finding eleven strange ostraca—different from any of the other inscribed pieces of pottery found. On each of them was a single name. All appeared to be written by the same hand. One of the names was Eleazar ben Yair, the leader of the zealots!

Yadin was convinced that he had not only come across the name of the leader, but also the names of the fateful ten who had performed the grim execution. I was present at Hebrew University, as a guest of doctors G. Ernest Wright and Nelson Glueck, when Dr. Yadin made his official report in a memorable, illustrated lecture. The audience will long remember the suspense and breathless silence as the hero of the expedition told about this dramatic discovery.

Some of the ancient storerooms were excavated; others were left just as they were when first approached by the archaeologists. The storerooms gave evidence of weapons sufficient to care for an army of ten thousand men. In the nearby bathhouse, near the skeleton of a zealot warrior, silvered scales of armor were found.

The most spectacular part of King Herod's work at Masada was the three-tiered villa, perched on the side of the massive cliff like three eagles' nests. The architects designed a palace citadel for the pompous king such as few kings have ever enjoyed. Steps have been created on the side of the perpendicular ridge that take the most intrepid enthusiasts down to the lower villa.

Near the foot of Masada is a small burial ground, where bones of some of the zealots were buried. Soldiers being inducted into the Israeli army today are brought to this site and repeat the solemn pledge, "Masada shall not fall again."

Yadin was attracted to this site to determine, if possible,

the credibility of Josephus. He came away with high scores for the noted historian. Today the writings of Josephus are regarded with a respect not known before. Concerning Yadin's work at Masada, Magan Broshi, curator of the Shrine of the Book, Israel Museum, writes:

> With all his [Josephus'] faults and apologetic traits, it can be proven in almost all cases that can be checked against actual finds that he is correct, sometimes amazingly so, when it comes to the archaeological data.[3]

The excavations of Caesarea and Masada, along with the testimony of the Dead Sea Scrolls, have all demonstrated Josephus's reliability.

Jerusalem treasures uncovered

Josephus also gives us a detailed account of the amazing work of Herod at Jerusalem, as well as a vivid account of the destruction of the city in A.D. 70. Here again, the archaeologists have proved him correct.

At the temple site in Jerusalem, Herod the great builder demonstrated his greatest skill and reached his crowning achievement. In 20 B.C., Herod began enlarging the temple mount to 350 acres. He then began the enlargement and beautification of the temple, a project that was not completed until A.D. 66, four years before it was destroyed.

Josephus describes Herod's temple as "the most prodigious work that was ever heard of by man." The king taught a thousand priests the building trade so that they could construct the holy of holies. He employed ten thousand skilled masons and used one thousand wagons to haul the stones from the quarries.

The inside measurements of the temple, with its holy and most holy place, were the same size as Solomon's temple; the outside courts, however, were doubled in size. During construction, one section was taken down at a time and rebuilt before continuing with another so that the sacred services could continue uninterrupted. Within the holy of holies, a large stone slab, or perhaps a gold slab, was placed where the ark of the covenant containing the Ten Commandments once stood.

The first project of the Jews, following the Six-Day War in June of 1967—which gave them access to the western wall—was clearing the area adjacent to the wall and converting it into a large plaza for worship and national celebrations. The western wall is the familiar "Wailing Wall," where, through the centuries, when political conditions would permit, the Jews have come to wail over the destruction of the temple and pray for its restoration.

Mazar digs at the western wall

Early in 1968, Dr. Benjamin Mazar, in behalf of the Israel Exploration Society and the Hebrew University of Jerusalem, began excavating the area below the western wall to the right of the plaza. The work continued for ten years. It is the most ambitious archaeological project ever attempted in Israel.[4]

King Solomon constructed a level platform on the highest hill of Jerusalem, upon which he erected the temple. To support the fill in this platform, he built a large retaining wall. Herod doubled the area of the platform by building new walls on three sides and by extending the eastern wall on the fourth side.

During Mazar's excavations below the western wall, seven courses of giant Herodian ashlars (stones) were uncovered, and bedrock was still sixty-eight feet below the surface. Mazar uncovered nineteen courses of giant building blocks in this area. In several places this took excavators down to the Herodian streets, the very streets Jesus walked on with His disciples.

Also, lying on the main north-south street adjacent to the western wall, the excavators found huge stones dating back to the destruction inflicted by the Roman general Titus in A.D. 70. Mazar chose to leave them just as they were found, piled on top of each other, as grim reminders of the holocaust that then struck the city.

The stones of this mighty retaining wall are of colossal proportions, several of them as much as thirty-five feet long and weighing seventy tons. The largest of them all is an impressive forty-seven feet long, ten feet high, thirteen feet thick, with a weight of approximately four hundred tons. Most of the stones are two to five tons. Many are ten tons or more. The stones were so precisely cut that no mortar was needed when fitting them together.

Mazar's work took him also to the area below the southern wall, where he uncovered the monumental staircase, 210 feet across, that led into the temple complex in the time of Christ. The exposed Herodian wall, fourteen courses of which he cleared, revealed where the double and triple gates had been. These gates led into the Royal Stoa that Herod had built on the southern end of the temple mount.

Josephus describes the stoa as having the shape of a basilica with four rows of forty columns, each fifty feet high, and so thick that it required three men with outstretched arms to reach around one of them. Jesus probably drove out the moneychangers from this stoa (see Mark 11:15-17; Luke 19:45, 46).

A prize find was a large eight-foot-long stone found near the southwest corner, bearing the inscription, "to the place of trumpeting to . . ." Although part is missing, it had obviously pointed toward a spot on top of the temple wall, fifty feet above the level of the court. Josephus describes this spot as the place where the priest stood to announce the beginning and ending of the Sabbath.[5]

The present walls reach their greatest height at the southeast corner of the temple mount, where they tower eighty feet into the sky. Exploratory trenches reveal that the foundation stones were placed on bedrock, ninety feet below the surface, making the present wall an incredible 170 feet high. Ninety-three feet below ground, excavators found a stone fourteen feet long, which they believed to be the chief cornerstone.

As seen today, the temple area is surrounded by massive walls built in 1542 during the Turkish reign of Sultan Suleiman, called the Magnificent. The lower portions, however, are the work of Herod. A seam in the wall, 106 feet north of the southeast corner, gives striking evidence that the wall to the south of this point was the work of Herod, when he enlarged the temple platform. Recent excavations north of the seam have led those doing the work to believe that the stones there were laid by King Solomon.[6] This contention, however, is still under debate.

The destruction of Jerusalem

During the passover season of A.D. 70, Titus, the Roman general, and sixty thousand trained soldiers came against the city. Over a million Jews crowded the precincts of the temple, having come to celebrate the sacred service. The destruction that followed is one of the bloodiest examples of human butchery. Titus tried to spare the temple, but a soldier threw a lighted torch through a window, setting it on fire. The entire city was ravaged and its population either slain or taken captive.

Archaeologists digging in the upper city of Jerusalem in January 1971 uncovered a house that had been destroyed by fire at the time. The skeleton of a woman was found where she was caught in her kitchen. The flames were fed by oil, and there was no escape.[7]

1. Robert J. Bull, "Caesarea Maritima—The Search for Herod's City," *BAR*, May/June 1982, 24-40; Robert L. Hohlfelder, "Caesarea Beneath the Sea," ibid., 42-52; Janet Crisler, "Caesarea World Monument," ibid., 41; Robert L. Hohlfelder, "Herod the Great's City on the Sea," *National Geographic*, February 1987.

2. Yigael Yadin, *Masada* (New York: Random House, 1966).

3. Magan Broshi, in review of *Flavius Josephus Between Jerusalem and Rome—His Life, His Works and Their Importance*, BAR, September/October 1990, 8.

4. Hershel Shanks, "Excavating in the Shadow of the Temple Mount," *BAR*, November/December 1986, 20-38. See also Meir Ben-Dov, "Herod's Mighty Temple Mount," ibid., 40-49; Kathleen and Leen Ritmeyer, "Reconstructing Herod's Temple Mount in Jerusalem," ibid., November/December 1989, 23-42; Leen Ritmeyer, "Quarrying and Transporting Stones for Herod's Temple Mount," ibid., 46-48; Kathleen and Leen Ritmeyer, "Reconstructing the Triple Gate," ibid., 49-53.

5. Aaron Demsky, "When the Priests Trumpeted the Onset of the Sabbath," *BAR*, November/December 1986, 50-52.

6. Ernest-Marie Laperrousaz, "King Solomon's Wall Still Supports the Temple Mount," *BAR*, May/June 1987, 34-44.

7. Nahman Avigad, "Jerusalem in Flames—the Burnt House Captures a Moment in Time," *BAR*, November/December 1983, 66-72.

Chapter 23

Light From the Dead Sea Scrolls

Amazing light has been cast on the New Testament period by the discovery of the Dead Sea Scrolls, considered the most important manuscript discovery of the century. The first scrolls were discovered in 1947. They are the product of a community of Essenes, religious hermits, who inhabited the old abandoned fort of Khirbet Qumran.

While visiting Qumran for the first time in 1957 with Dr. Siegfried Horn, I observed the excavations that had been underway since 1951. Bronze coins were found, dating from the beginning of the Christian era to the time of the Jewish revolt that ended in the destruction of Jerusalem. The dates on the coins and other evidence indicate that, as the Roman legions swept down on the Qumran community, the inhabitants hastily chucked the scrolls in jars and hid them in the caves, no doubt hoping to recover them later.

On the second floor of a tower that dominates the area, the archaeologists found the remains of a brick table about sixteen feet long and twenty inches high. Nearby were parts of two shorter tables. On the tables were three inkstands, one of bronze and the others of clay. They had uncovered the scriptorium, the very rooms in which the manuscripts were written.

Several cisterns were discovered, one of which had apparently served as a baptismal pool. A crack in the steps leading down into it was no doubt caused by the severe earthquake of 31 B.C. reported by Josephus.

In addition to Cave 1, where the first scrolls were found, forty additional caves produced thirty-five thousand scroll fragments from four hundred manuscripts, including parts of every book of the Old Testament except Esther. In the total collection, the Pentateuch, or five books of Moses, were most widely represented, followed by Isaiah, the Psalms, Daniel, and Jeremiah. There were also commentaries on the Psalms, Isaiah, and some of the minor prophets, along with many nonbiblical documents.

Dr. Joseph Saad, curator of the Rockefeller Museum, escorted us over the area of the excavations. In Jerusalem, he took us into the scrollery of the Rockefeller Museum, where the work of putting all the fragments together was going on— the world's greatest jigsaw puzzle.

The Essenes

The Essenes who inhabited the region were one of the three principal Jewish sects of that day—the others were the Pharisees and Sadducees. Josephus often refers to the Essenes in his writings. He regarded them very highly. Of them he wrote, "They exceed all other men who addict themselves to virtue."

Based on a total population of about 1.5 million people living in Palestine at the time, it has been estimated that there were four thousand Essenes, six thousand Pharisees, and three thousand Sadducees. Separated from the world at Qumran, the Essenes lived in a well-organized community, guided by rigid rules and strict discipline, organized into groups with a priest over each group.

The Essenes' organization and rules appear in their *Manual of Discipline*, which was also found at Qumran. They withdrew from the world, going into the desert to prepare the way of the Lord by the study of the Torah. And, at Qumran, they meticulously transcribed these precious documents. They believed that they were the true people of God and that they possessed the only true interpretation of Scripture.

The scrolls speak of a "Teacher of Righteousness" who founded the community, and of his conflict with a Wicked Priest. Also, of a war between the "Sons of Light" and the "Sons of Darkness." They believed that they were living in "the last days," described by the Old Testament prophets. They lived a life of prayer and expectation of the coming of the Messiah, who would save the righteous and judge the wicked in the final war on evil.

It is an amazing fact, and a powerful confirmation of Christianity, that when the true Messiah, Jesus Christ, did appear, it was at the right time and in fulfillment of literally hundreds of Old Testament prophecies in which many striking details of His life were foretold centuries before His birth.

The biblical scrolls

Important as are the nonbiblical manuscripts, the most significant are the biblical scrolls found at Qumran. These range from the complete scroll of Isaiah and the Psalms to fragments of other books. There were also writings containing commentaries and references to the Scriptures. We can understand the sensational nature of the great discovery when we realize that these biblical manuscripts are a thousand years older than any others known before, except for one small fragment known as the Nash Papyrus that contains a portion of the book of Deuteronomy, dating from the first century B.C.

The Scriptures today are based on a common text developed in the eighth and ninth century A.D. by a group of scribes known as the Masoretes. Their work is known as the "Masoretic" text. They took the text that had been handed down and divided it into sections, adding vowels, signs, accents, and punctuation.

The big question often asked is, How can we know that the Masoretic text and the translations based on it are the same as the originals that were written many long centuries before?

"Surely," said the critics, "the scribes and copyists must have made mistakes. What we have can't possibly be the same as what was originally written."

Before the discovery of the Dead Sea Scrolls, there was, in fact, no way to prove that the doubters were wrong. Furthermore, it seemed very unlikely that such evidence would ever be found. Sir Frederick Kenyon, a leading authority on the ancient texts, in his highly regarded work, *Our Bible and the Ancient Manuscripts*, published in 1948, wrote:

> There is, indeed, no probability that we shall ever find manuscripts of the Hebrew text going back to a period before the formation of the text which we know as Masoretic.[1]

But, amazing as it may seem, at the very time these words were published, the first of the scrolls from Qumran were coming to light. And as these priceless documents were studied, to the great surprise of the critics, the ancient texts were found to be virtually the same as the Masoretic text and, therefore, the same as the text of the Bible we have today.

The evidence was in—to a degree scarcely dreamed possible! This new discovery at Qumran did more to change the attitude of the critics toward the Bible than any other discovery of all time.

Learned scholars who questioned the accuracy of the Bible had often tried to improve on the text by making what they considered necessary corrections, called emendations. Now, with the ancient manuscripts before them, they could see that the originals were correct after all, and that their so-called improvements were in error.

The Bible is no ordinary book. Not only is the amazing preservation of the true text a remarkable evidence of God's providential care, but it is equally providential that the scrolls were hidden away in the one place in the world where they could survive the ages—the lowest spot on earth. In any other environment, they would have long since perished. But at Qumran they were protected in caves in a bone-dry area, a place that was surely prepared by an omniscient God.

God's hand must also have been over the timing of the discovery. For it was not until the rise of the higher school of biblical criticism in the eighteenth century that the authenticity and authority of the Bible was seriously questioned. When the evidence was most needed, the amazing discovery was made.

Finding the scrolls proved valuable in many ways. They revealed that our Bible of today is absolutely accurate and reliable. They demonstrated that the book of Isaiah was considered the work of one author in the third century B.C. They lend support to the early authorship of the book of Daniel. They shed light on the history and culture of the time of Jesus.

Of special interest is the so-called Temple Scroll, at twenty-seven feet, the longest of all the scrolls. Although first discovered in 1956, it didn't come to light until the Six-Day War of June 1967, when it came into the possession of Dr. Yigael Yadin. Although the Temple Scroll dates back to the middle of the first century A.D., the original composition is believed to date back to about 150-125 B.C.

According to Yadin, this scroll contains the basic Torah, or law, of the Essenes, and as such was regarded as sacred. Although it includes long passages of Scripture, mostly from the books of Moses, nearly half of it postulates elaborate plans for the building of the temple. It also describes the sacrificial service of the temple, as well as the laws of the city of the temple.[2]

Today the vast majority of the scrolls, about seven hundred patched-together manuscripts, are still housed in the Rockefeller Museum in Jerusalem. The work of editing and publishing them continues under an international team. The work has gone so slowly as to arouse considerable criticism. However, encouraging word came in March 1991, with the announcement by Emanuel Tov of Jerusalem's Hebrew University, a leading editor of the scrolls, to a news conference at the close of the International Congress on the Dead Sea Scrolls in El Escorial, Spain, that an expanded team of young scholars, working with computers, hopes to publish all the scrolls by 1996.[3]

Since that announcement, a major breakthrough came in September 1991, with the announcement of the Huntington Library of Pasadena, California, that they were making their library of negatives of the unpublished scrolls available to all scholars. Subsequent to this, the Biblical Archaeological Society, publisher of *Biblical Archaeological Review*, announced the publication of a two-volume set of the previously unpublished scrolls in *A Facsimile Edition of the Dead Sea Scrolls*.

The Biblical Archaeological Society has also established an Institute for Dead Sea Scroll Studies to "facilitate the dissemination and exchange of information and research materials concerning the Dead Sea Scrolls among all scholars."[4]

The relatively complete scrolls are displayed in the beautiful Shrine of the Book, a museum constructed for this purpose on the campus of Israel Museum in Jerusalem.

All one in Christ

A major message from the scrolls, particularly the Temple Scroll, is that Christianity and Judaism were more closely related than previously thought. As a result, New Testament scholars now recognize an increased indebtedness to the Old Testament and are learning Hebrew; and Old Testament scholars have taken a new interest in New Testament studies.

The New Testament and Christianity are now seen as an outgrowth and a continuation of the Judaism of the Old Testament. After all, Jesus and all His disciples were Jews. All of the first Christians were Jews. The question was not, Can Jews become Christians? but, Can Gentiles become Christians?

When a Jew becomes a Christian today, he becomes a

complete Jew, for he accepts Jesus, the true Jewish Messiah, foretold by all the Jewish prophets of the Old Testament.

And Gentiles, when they become Christians, become true Jews.

As Paul states it:

> He is not a Jew, which is one outwardly; . . . but he is a Jew, which is one inwardly. . . . For they are not all Israel, which are of Israel: neither, because they are the seed of Abraham, are they all children (Romans 2:28, 29; 9:6, 7).

Archaeology, then, has a part in answering these important questions: Who are the true Israel? Who are the true Jews? All who are true children of God. Paul declares:

> Ye all are the children of God by faith in Christ Jesus. For as many of you as have been baptized into Christ have put on Christ. There is neither Jew nor Greek . . . for ye are all one in Christ Jesus. And if ye be Christ's, then are ye Abraham's seed, and heirs according to the promise (Galatians 3:26-29).

In the light of the Dead Sea Scrolls, Christians can now appreciate more fully their indebtedness to the Jews of the Old Testament. Jews can now better understand Christianity as a continuation and fulfillment of their greatest hopes—hopes centered in the true Messiah, who was sent to be the Saviour of all humankind.

Jerusalem—the old and the new

Today true Christians, whether Jew or Gentile, share in the great hope of Abraham and other heroes of the Scriptures. They regarded themselves as pilgrims, sojourners, on this earth. They looked forward to a new heaven and a new earth as their eternal home.

These all died in faith, not having received the promises, but having seen them afar off, and were persuaded of them, and embraced them, and confessed that they were strangers and pilgrims on the earth. . . . But now they desire a better country, that is, an heavenly: wherefore God is not ashamed to be called their God: for he hath prepared for them a city (Hebrews 11:13, 16).

Speaking of Abraham, we read, "He looked for a city which hath foundations, whose builder and maker is God" (Hebrews 11:10).

Today we look beyond the earthly Jerusalem. Like the biblical heroes, we look in faith to the New Jerusalem, that city in the sky. John, as a prisoner on the island of Patmos, was shown that city and described it in the book of Revelation, chapters 21 and 22.

Before Christ ascended to heaven following His resurrection, He made the precious promise:

I go to prepare a place for you. And if I go and prepare a place for you, I will come again, and receive you unto myself; that where I am, there ye may be also (John 14:2, 3).

Jesus will keep His word. He is coming back to earth to receive His own. His promise is:

Behold, I come quickly; and my reward is with me, to give every man according as his work shall be. . . . Blessed are they that do his commandments, that they may have right to the tree of life, and may enter in through the gates into the city. . . . And the Spirit and the bride say, Come. And let him that heareth say, Come. And let him that is athirst come. And whosoever will, let him take the water of life freely.

. . . He which testifieth these things saith, Surely I come quickly. Amen. Even so, come, Lord Jesus (Revelation 22:12, 14, 17, 20).

May the treasures of archaeology, uncovered from the sands of time, help make us more ready for that day.

---

1. Sir Frederick Kenyon, *Our Bible and the Ancient Manuscripts,* 4th ed. (New York: Harper & Brothers, 1951), 48.

2. Yigael Yadin, "The Temple Scroll—the Longest and Most Recently Discovered Dead Sea Scroll," *BAR*, September/October 1984, 33-49.

3. Associated Press in the *Fresno Bee*, 22 March 1991.

4. *BAR*, January/February 1992, 63, 64.

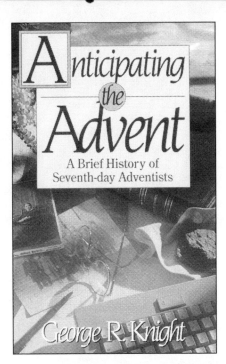

When anticipating a grand event, it's hard to contain your excitement. This was how the Millerites felt as October 22, 1844, drew near. But hopes were dashed as the day of promise came and went without sight of their beloved Saviour.

Anticipating the Advent: A Brief History of Seventh-day Adventists is the story of how a small group of people who believed in the imminent return of Christ came to view themselves as a prophetic people with a responsibility to take their unique message to all the world. Author and church historian George R. Knight captures the enthusiasm and sorrow of the Great Disappointment, revisits the days of early Adventist history, and brings us up to date on the church today.

Must reading for those who want to discover their spiritual and prophetic roots.

US$8.95/Cdn$10.75

Available now at your local ABC, or call toll free 1-800-765-6955.

© Pacific Press Publishing Association 2615